LEADERSHIP LESSONS FROM GREAT WORLD LEADERS

Fred M. Lang, Ph.D.

american press

60 State Street #700
Boston, Massachusetts 02109
www.americanpresspublishers.com

358
LAN
5-31-18

Dedication

I want to dedicate this book to my wife, Susan, who served as a sounding board during the four years of research and writing. She was always available for opinions and reactions to each of the chapters. I would not have been able to complete this work without her invaluable encouragement and assistance.

Susan, who is an accomplished artist, also agreed to draw the original sketches for the ten leaders profiled. My thanks go to her for lending her talent to this project.

ACKNOWLEDGEMENTS

There are two people, who I need to acknowledge, who contributed their talents to the publication of this book. The first is Paul Terry who was the former Vice President of Blackboard, Inc. in Washington, D.C. Paul wrote the wonderful **Foreword** for this book. He demonstrated his confidence in me by hiring me as a consultant to Blackboard. During the four years that I worked with Paul, I came to know a man who had a passion for learning. He recognized that platforms like Blackboard helped the learner to take a deeper cognitive dive into a subject than was not available through any other virtual medium. We teamed up to jointly share the master of ceremonies function for the Federal Workshops, which grew in numbers each of the years in which they were held. Our business relationship grew into a friendship that was underscored by a deep respect for the skills that he brought to the table. I am humbled and honored by his kind words in the Foreword.

Secondly, I want to thank Dr. Lucy Franks who is my co-instructor for the Bellevue University on-line doctoral course entitled: **Leadership Theory**. She is not only a wonderful instructor, but she has become a valued collaborator and friend. She provided her editorial assistance to fine-tune this publication, which was greatly appreciated. She has also shown her confidence in me by using this book as an integral element in the course, **Leadership Seminar**. She recognized that this book helps to demonstrate the application of leadership through the profiles of the lives of great world leaders. I deeply appreciate the trust that she has in me.

FOREWORD

I vividly remember the first time I had the privilege of meeting Dr. Fred Lang. Our paths crossed at a gathering of human capital leaders in Washington DC. Fred mixed easily within that environment. Understandable given that he founded and, for the first five years, chaired the Federal Inter-Agency Chief Learning Officers Council, a distinguished group of senior Training Officers within the U.S. federal government who are collectively responsible for the training and development of over 2.5 million federal employees.

As a mutual acquaintance introduced us, Fred immediately recognized the leading software company (Blackboard) I helped lead and noted the software's unique ability in helping facilitate cognitive learning. While his stellar reputation already preceded him, I was impressed with his firm grasp and description of the software's capability. The phrase "cognitive learning" did not appear in any of the company's marketing materials. Yet that capability, in my mind, was what truly distinguished the offering in the marketplace and made it the market leader. While Fred had some exposure to the product in the past, assessing software functionality was by no means his area of expertise. Within 30 seconds of meeting him, he displayed an ability to both grasp its significance and succinctly describe it better than anyone else I have ever met, either before or since. Fred has used that gift of succinct, thoughtful insight throughout this book.

Since that encounter, I had the good fortune to work more closely with Fred. In particular, he and I served as co-hosts of a biannual gathering of leaders in Washington DC which we started. That gathering grew with each passing meeting in part because collaboration and the sharing of ideas come so naturally to Fred.

While I worked with many Fortune 500 companies and large scale organizations with their leadership development efforts, I continue to learn from this book. For example, Fred shares with us how passion and commitment do not distinguish between the rich or the poor. Although Margaret Thatcher was the daughter of a poor English shop-keeper and Alexander the Great was the son of a Macedonian king, both made their mark in history as great leaders with solid backgrounds of achievement.

In the chapters that follow, Fred draws upon a wide range of historical figures as well as historical references, including Plutarch and the speech given prior to the Battle of Agincourt in Shakespeare's play Henry the Fifth. Fred includes insights from women of historical significance, including Elizabeth I and Golda Meir. He weaves in anecdotes, such as how and why the term leadership was introduced into our collective vocabulary.

All of Fred's many traits—leader, teacher, collaborator, and visionary—shine through in this book. Via the literary use of storytelling of a historical figure's life, Fred takes us on a journey through history so that we can observe those leadership attributes that enabled these great leaders to leave their mark in our history of the world. By identifying and summarizing the attributes of leaders and leadership, he helps crystalize for the reader the essential elements for his or her own success. To further enable our learning, he provides both questions for reflection as well as ideas for how to achieve the professional goals you seek.

I trust you will find Dr. Lang's insights and analysis in the pages that follow as helpful as I have over the many years I have had the good fortune to know him.

Paul Terry
(former) Blackboard Executive
Leading authority in learning and training technology

CONTENTS

Chapter 1 – Introduction 1

Chapter 2 – Creating the Future 5

Chapter 3 – Leadership Attribute 15

Chapter 4 – Alexander the Great..................................... 27

Chapter 5 – Elizabeth I 41

Chapter 6 – Peter the Great 55

Chapter 7 – George Washington 65

Chapter 8 – Winston Churchill.. 79

Chapter 9 – Golda Meir... 93

Chapter 10 – Napoléon Bonaparte 105

Chapter 11 – Catherine the Great 119

Chapter 12 – Martin Luther King, Jr. 131

Chapter 13 – Margaret Thatcher 145

Chapter 14 – Thoughts & Reflections 159

Chapter 1
INTRODUCTION

For over 25 years, I taught management and leadership, as an adjunct professor, at the graduate and doctoral levels for three universities. During this time, my career in management began in the public sector as an assistant to a city manager, but soon transitioned into the private sector after four years. After a number of years, I became a Vice-President for Business Development for a California consulting firm; a Director of Sales and Marketing for a Silicon Valley firm; and then founded a consulting business on the west coast. While all of these changes were taking place in my life, I also served in the Oregon National Guard and as a commanding officer in the California Army National Guard.

Years later, my career seemed to boomerang back once again into the public sector. After assuming a number of leadership positions, I eventually became the Chief Learning Officer and Director of Training, in the Office of the Secretary, for the U.S. Department of Commerce in Washington, D.C. The Department of Commerce is composed of over 46,000 employees and 13 separate bureaus. As my leadership responsibilities increased over the years, I struggled with various leadership strategies that would fit the many public and private sector organizations in which I found myself.

I wanted, as do those who are reading this book, to be the best leader that I could become. Although I studied leadership concepts and read many leadership books in order to help me realize my full potential, I felt that there was still something missing and knew that—possibly—I could learn something from the great leaders who marked their place in history. I decided to research their lives and their ideas, which led to the writing of this book.

After doing an initial year of research for this book, I began to put into words my thoughts about leadership and the attributes that bring real meaning to this word. There have been so many books written about the subject of leadership that it would be easy for this book to be lost in the cacophony created by the world library on this subject. Let there be no mistake; there have been many wonderful and inspiring books written on the subject of leadership. However, I would suggest to you that you will find this book much different from anything that you have ever read before on leadership. If you like reading history and you want to understand the concepts of leadership as the great leaders from world history employed them and excel as a leader, you will enjoy reading this book.

The purpose of writing this book is to thoughtfully examine the essential observable leadership attributes that make all the difference in genuine leadership. I will do this in ways that brings to life, through storytelling, ten historical figures throughout the ages that have gone down in the annals of history as exemplary leaders. I wanted to discover what leadership attributes gave them their place in the history of the world. Each historical figure is rated against specific leadership attributes so that you can make sense out of their experiences and then apply them to your own study of how to best lead within your organization.

This book can serve as a reference to, not only the leadership attributes that will be introduced to the reader, but it will undoubtedly trigger many discussions about the essential elements of leadership and how they were applied in various situations and historical periods. Through storytelling; through a sense of personal reflection; and through discussion, we can learn to become better leaders in our organizations. We must learn from past leaders or we may be destined to repeat their mistakes.

I selected leaders from ancient and contemporary history that represent many countries and both genders. I have always felt that the female gender is under represented in leadership discussions and I wanted to be more inclusive in this work. In addition, these leaders are drawn from multiple categories including: kings and queens, the military, presidents and statesmen, and reformer/activists. Through a process of storytelling, we will discover what observable leadership attributes helped them to make their mark in history.

Finally, you will learn how you can apply, what you have learned from the past, to your own leadership challenges. Whether your organization is in the public sector, the private sector, or the military, these leader profiles will help you to hone your leadership skills and become the best that you can become. This book was written for you, regardless of the experience and background that you bring to your career. It is not who you are, but who you can become.

Read and enjoy the journey!

Chapter 2
CREATING THE FUTURE

"Leadership is the art of creating the future"
Dr. Fred Lang

Throughout recorded history, we were introduced to many leaders. We read about Moses and how he led the Israelites out of Egypt and across the Sinai Desert and into the Promised Land. We also marveled at the exploits of Alexander the Great and how he conquered the known world during his time. The exploits, conquests, and defeat of Napoleon Bonaparte are central to France's history. The world was gripped with fear as they waited for the outcome of Winston Churchill's test of leadership during the struggle to hold England and the European community together against Hitler and the Third Reich. In more recent times, we witnessed the extraordinary leadership of Dr. Martin Luther King during the epoch civil rights movement in the mid-20th Century.

The Subject of Leadership

The subject of **Leadership** has been the focus of many stories and books during the 19th and 20th centuries that attempted to define the characteristics of a leader. These authors have examined the lives of great men and women and attempted to discover what set each of them apart from their followers. Was it the force of their personality? Was it their special skills or characteristics? Was it their vision that each communicated to their followers? Was it the situation in which they found themselves? Or, was it something else that caused them to rise to a position of leadership? What common threads ran through the lives of the great leaders?

The word: "Leader" did not appear in the English language until about the year 1300 AD.[1] It was not introduced into our collective vocabulary until the first half of the 19th century when reference was first made in various publications related to political influence with respect to the British Parliament. Prior to that time, many other words were used to describe leadership, which included: king, head of state, queen, military commander, Roman Proconsul, and chief.

Leadership Theories

A number of leadership theories were researched and discussed by many leading academicians over the past century to try to explain why and how a leader emerges. However, none of these theories fully account for all relevant variables that try to explain leaders and how they lead. In the following, you will read about some of the more prominent theories.

The **Great-Man Theory** put forth the proposition that leaders are born, not made. This theory would account for the great kings and queens, military commanders, and

---

1 Bernard, p. 11.

statesman who tended to shape history through their extra-ordinary actions and vision. Alexander the Great, Julius Caesar, and Elizabeth I are examples of this theory. However, it falls short when you realize that some notables in history were severely limited by their own lack of talent and ability. In other words, their part of the world was only changed by their limited ability to have a grand vision and execute change.

Another model is referred to as the **Trait Theory** of leadership. This theory examines the characteristics and the attributes of leaders to explain why some leaders made such an impact in their historical landscape. It was believed that some of these personality traits were part of the personal heredity of the leader, but this theory once again fell short in its inability to fully account for the environmental aspect of training and mentoring. As an example, Alexander the Great was mentored by Aristotle[2]. Plutarch's book: *Parallel lives of Noble Grecians and Romans*, which was written in the first century AD, describes the common virtues and failings of pairs of similar Greeks and Romans.[3] There were a number of traits identified by many who researched this issue and tried to link traits to leadership.

Servant Leadership is a theory originally expounded by Greenleaf[4] in his book with the same name. The Servant Leader can be referred to as a steward who oversees property and assets owned by the public. This could be most

---

[2] Dupuy, p. 27.
[3] Rogers, p. 109.
[4] Greenleaf, *Servant Leadership*.

any leader who *serves* the people in a governmental agency. However, an expanded definition is one who leads by listening to his/her followers and by empathizing with their needs and concerns. The Servant Leader helps them to achieve their goals and in the process also achieves the goals of the leader. In a more contemporary setting, the servant leader can be seen as one who provides the support and the coaching for his/her employees so that they can be successful and, in the process, the leader also becomes successful.

As a way of accounting for all variables and filling in the gap toward a more universal theory of leadership, the **Contingency Leadership Theories** were postulated. One sub-type theory that merged was the Situational Leadership Theory. This theory offered the explanation that leaders emerge in history when the situation calls for them. When a situational crisis becomes evident, a leader seems to emerge with all of the right skills and attributes. Winston Churchill, Prime Minister of England during World War II, and Franklin Roosevelt, the President of the United States during the same period of time, are illustrations of this theory.

One of the more recent descriptions of a leader in the late 20th Century and the early 21st Century is that of a **Transformational Leader**. This is a leader who leads his/her followers to accomplish major changes in institutions and organizations. These changes could be the result of major paradigm shifts in the direction and vision of an organization or simply a change in a process or production of a product or service. These leaders see opportunities to improve an aspect of an organization and lead their followers or team to bring it about. Russia's Peter the Great brought civility and education to a backward country while conducting a major transformation of its government and administrative systems. In more contemporary times, let us focus upon the mighty Intel Corporation. When Andy Grove, the CEO of Intel, led his company away from producing lucrative memory chips to producing high-risk silicon micro processing chips, he became a major transformational leader of his company and, in the process, defined an entirely new industry.

It is important to understand that leaders cannot be reliably identified with one leadership theory, but with elements of many leadership theories. Leaders are multifaceted and employ different approaches to fit the situation in which they encounter. Through an understanding of a variety of approaches to leadership, the leader can become most effective in achieving his/her objectives.

Arriving at a definition of leadership is not as easy as it may seem. Even though we can reflect upon the past and how it was applied, it is indeed a moving target. After decades of academic research and over 350 definitions, it is not entirely clear as to the distinction between a leader and a follower. Bennis & Nanus write: "Most of these definetions don't agree with each other, and many of them would seem quite remote to the leaders whose skills are being dissected. Definitions reflect fads, fashions, political tides and academic trends."[5]

We could attempt to define leadership by referencing some common characteristics, which surface in many of its

---

[5] Bennis & Nanus, pp. 4-5.

multiple definitions. In exercising the role, the leader attempts:

to influence an outcome
to lead followers
to enforce compliance
to set up a power relationship
to paint a vision or goal for followers
to direct multiple and diverse agendas into one common
agenda

Leadership Attributes

So we ask ourselves, what are the attributes or common threads that are observable in a superior leader? This is not an easy question to answer. There does not seem to be any consensus as to what specific attributes are parts of the psychological makeup of superior leaders.

During the four years in which the author conducted research for this book, many books and the Internet were surveyed while searching for a list, or compilation, or even opinions about leadership attributes. Although the author was seeking a consensus about the most critical leadership attributes, it was never found. So, in recognizing a general absence of consensus from many of the extraordinary authors that wrote about the subject of leadership, each instance was recorded in which a characteristic was cited. The number of occurrences was summed up and the top attributes were selected which were referenced most frequently. In conducting this summary validation process, similar ideas were combined into six major themes that figured prominently into the writing of this book. The six leadership attributes that the author discovered through this process are:

INTEGRITY
RISK TAKER
COMMUNICATION
PASSION
VISION
RESILIENCY

A word about the leaders selected for this book is necessary at this point. The author avoided selecting any religious leader so as not to offend anyone who may be a member of a religion or religious sect that could have been inadvertently omitted. Also, all of the leaders profiled in this book have passed into history and their accomplishments are left for the ages and open to all to study. Finally, a word about morality and ethics is appropriate. Morality and ethics are dictated by the norms of the period in which the profiled leader lived. Many of those profiled in this book were leaders at a time of intense war and world conflict. The morality and ethical actions of some may be seen differently through the lens of distant times and centuries. It is for this reason that the author only focused upon leadership attributes and explored their affect on the great leaders profiled in this book. The purpose of this book is to profile and rate these leaders against a set of attributes so that contemporary leaders can learn how to become better leaders.

This book offers ratings of each leader profiled; chapter conclusions; interpretive lessons for leaders; and questions for reflection that will help the reader think more deeply about the profiled leaders and how their skills may be applied to your own leadership inventory. Read each profile and learn what you can apply to your own leadership strategy. None of these profiled leaders are so similar that any of them can be seen as carbon copies of the ideal leader. Each leader is unique and brings different skills to the table, but there are similarities.

References

Bass, Bernard. (1990). The meaning of leadership in Bass & Stogdill's *Handbook of leadership*. Third edition. New York: *The Free Press*. p. 11.

Bennis, Warren & Burt Nanus. (1985). *Leaders the strategies for taking charge*. New York: Harper & Row. pp. 4-5.

Dupuy, Trevor N. (1995). *The harper encyclopedia of military biography*. New York: Harper Collins Publishers. p .27.

Greenleaf, Robert K. (1991). *Servant leadership*. New Jersey: Paulist Press.

Grove, Andrew S. (1996). *Only the paranoid survive*. New York: Doubleday.

Rogers, Nigel. (2012). *The illustrated encyclopedia of ancient Greece*. Lorenz Books. p. 109.

Chapter 3
LEADERSHIP ATTRIBUTES

Leadership attributes are defined as those learned characteristics that influence the thought process and, thereby, drive the leader's behavior toward a worthwhile goal. However, it is not solely the leadership attributes that drive behavior, it is something much deeper. In the great leader, there is a genetic predisposition to lead that surfaces within their personality characteristics. It is this trigger that brings all of the leader's learned attributes into focus. It is particularly apparent during a crisis or when the situation arises that demands a leader.

If we examine this definition through another lens, it might make a lot more sense. Have you every known someone who was in the military and they told you that he comes from a long line of soldiers? Or, have you known an artist who boasts that she is only one of many in their family who are artists? Or what about the educator who hails from a long line of teachers? The soldier, the artist, and the educator must learn the skills to be good at their trade, but each is probably predisposed toward that line of work and that skill set. The passion to pursue a specific line of work is embedded in their DNA and triggers the engagement of the learned skills.

In this chapter, we will examine the SIX LEADERSHIP ATTRIBUTES that were discovered during earlier research for this book. We will also provide a working definition of each. In addition, a rating or evaluation schemata will be discussed that will be used with each leader profiled. At the end of each chapter, leadership lessons and reflective questions are discussed which are gleaned from each leader's profile.

Integrity

> *"Integrity is the first step to true greatness. Men love to praise, but are slow to practice it. To maintain it in high places costs self-denial; in all places it is liable to opposition, but its end is glorious, and the universe will yet do it homage."*[1]

C. Simmons

The first attribute is Integrity. This word implies a deep trust between the leader and the follower with regards to performing and behaving according to the expected norms of the times. It is the establishment of a bond of trust that is underscored with promises kept; expected and anticipated behavior; and generally living up to the character norms of the group. The leader must remain true to the group expectations and any violation of that trust will begin to deteriorate the relationship.

Norms and group expectations change with the times. Modes of dress and attire; ethics and morality; tolerance and acceptance have changed dramatically over the last

---

[1] Edwards, Tryon, C.N. Catrevas, Jonathan Edwards, & Ralph Browns. (1964). *The New Dictionary of Thoughts*. United States: Standard Book Co. (p.315)

century. Imagine what the changes might have been over the past 12 centuries. However, for a person to have integrity, he/she must be true to the norms of their period and the reasonable group expectations of behavior. Integrity is indeed a key attribute of all leaders.

Do not confuse integrity with ethics and morality. These characteristics represent the time in which the leader lives. Ethics and morality evolve over time just as they have within our own lifetime. Integrity is a timeless characteristic that bonds the leader with the follower. If a leader fails to live up to the expectations of his/her followers and the behavioral norms of the group, the bond becomes broken and integrity is lost.

Risk Taker

"We should never so entirely avoid danger as to appear irresolute and cowardly; but, at the same time, we should avoid unnecessarily exposing ourselves to danger, than which nothing can be more foolish"[2]

Cicero

Leaders take calculated risks in their tactics and in their strategies in order to achieve their visions. When the outcome of a leader's action is unknown, it is a risk that is being assessed. Every military, political, and reformist engagement is a risk relative to the desired outcome. Without risks taken, there is no advancement or progress in a

---

[2] Edwards, Tryon, C.N. Catrevas, Jonathan Edwards, & Ralph Browns. (1964). *The New Dictionary of Thoughts*. United States: Standard Book Co. (p. 127)

society. What would have happened if the Founding Fathers of the United States decided to play it safe and not revolt against England? What would have happened if England, during World War II, had decided to hope for the best and simply agree to Hitler's demands? What would have happened if the entrepreneurs of the world decided not to risk their fortunes and reputations on new ideas or inventions? A risk, by its very definition, indicates that the risk taken could end in failure. However, all great leaders have experienced some failures and that is how they learned what not to do. Risks are endemic to success.

Communication

"Words have a magical power. They can bring either the greatest happiness or deepest despair; can transfer knowledge from teacher to student; words enable the orator to sway his audience and dictate its decisions. Words are capable of arousing the strongest emotions and prompting all men's actions."

Sigmund Freud

Communication is a tool used by the leader to rally his/her followers; energize an audience; and generally bring out the deepest of emotions. Words, delivered in just the right way, can engender the deepest of love between two people and bring out deep sorrow when a eulogy is delivered. It is the tool used by extraordinary teachers who transfer knowledge to their students. It is the tool that can start and stop wars more effectively than any war machine.

The ability to communicate effectively is an absolute prerequisite of every leader. Who can forget the speech given in King Henry V, in Shakespeare's play of the same name, when he addresses his greatly outnumbered troops on the field of Battle at Agincourt on Saint Crispin's Day?

"… From this day to the ending of the world, but we in it shall be remembered, we few, we happy few, we band of brothers. For he today that sheds his blood with me shall be my brother…"[3]

Or think about the powerful words of Thomas Jefferson in the United States Declaration of Independence: "We hold these truths to be self-evident, that all men are created equal…". Or perhaps the words delivered by President John F. Kennedy during his Inauguration Address when he said: "Ask not what your country can do for you, but what you can do for your country?" These leaders were able to stir the emotions of their followers to action. The skillful ability to write and speak is a powerful tool of a leader.

Passion

"How many seemingly impossible things have been accomplished by resolute men because they had to do, or die."

Napoleon Bonaparte

Passion and determination echo the underpinnings of a great leader's attribute. A skillful leader will surely fail

---

[3] Shakespeare, *Henry the Fifth*, Act IV, Scene III (pp. 734-735)

without also having a deep passion and determination to succeed—in spite of the odds.

During the American Civil War, General George B. McClellan was appointed by President Abraham Lincoln to assume command of the Union Army of the Potomac. It was no wonder that the President made this appointment since McClellan graduated 2nd in his class from West Point. He also studied Napoleonic military tactics and wrote a book entitled the *Armies of Europe*. For all of his education, he was unable to advance his army into battle. Lincoln finally replaced him. Another union general by the name of Grant had an unremarkable career graduating near the bottom of his West Point class. However, it was his determination and passion to bring the Civil War to an end that Lincoln said: "I can't spare this man—he fights."

Vision

"When a leader uses words as a way of applying paint to a mental canvas describing a future state, the completed portrait can be compelling enough to rouse and energize followers to action."

Dr. Fred Lang

Vision is an essential element of every great leader. The leader's position in an organization is a unique one that allows him or her to see into a future state. Through the power of words, the leader conveys the strength of commitment and passion; a vision for the future; courage to lead; and empathy with followers. After being attacked by Germany during World War II, Prime Minister Winston

Churchill, addressed the people of England to give them hope and a resolve that England would not become a conquered nation. After the United States was attacked on December 7, 1941 by the Japanese Empire, the President of the United States, Franklin D. Roosevelt, addressed the American people to let them know that this unprovoked attack would not go unanswered. These are examples of two great leaders who roused their countries to action through the use of their powerful vision of a future state.

President John F. Kennedy, in a powerful speech delivered at Rice University on September 12, 1962, painted a grand vision for the American people. After reflecting upon the extraordinary advances that the human race has made within the past century, he proclaimed that the United States would send a man to the moon before the decade was out. At the time he delivered this speech, the technology and the metals that would be used in such a spacecraft, had not even been discovered. His vision launched an entire new industry that had not existed before.

Resiliency

"A resilient leader is able to recover from deep losses or disappointments and attempt a new strategy. Such a leader is focused and shrugs off their failure and demonstrates tenacity, courage, and belief in the new strategy to begin again to reach the desired goal."

Dr. Fred Lang

Resiliency is the ability to get back up after experiencing a serious defeat or disappointment and to re- engage toward the goal. Although there may be significant odds stacked against the outcome, the resilient leader develops a new strategy to obtain the desired goal.

Many emotions come to the surface that attempt to derail the journey to the goal. Some refer to themselves as victims while others sink into depression and inaction. Those that shrug these emotions away and move forward toward their goal, with a renewed sense of commitment, are the resilient leaders.

Elizabeth I of England (1558-1603) was faced with the terror of the Spanish Armada in 1588. King Phillip II of Spain wanted to dethrone her and capture England. At that time in history, Spain was the indisputable world naval power. The Queen stood her ground against overwhelming odds and rallied her troops on the shores of England while they watched the approaching fleet that was sent to devastate her country. Using a strategy of fireboats crashing into the oncoming Spanish fleet and an unanticipated terrific storm at sea, the day was won. Her resilient spirit won the victory for England. If she had given in to these derailment emotions, England might be quite different today.

Some Conclusions about Each Leader

After an examination of each profile, a score will be given for that Leader. This will be an imperfect attempt at assessing the leadership attributes of that leader. Although a number of historical sources were examined about each leader, unless one has first-hand knowledge of the profiled leader, it is very difficult to deliver an accurate score. However, for the purposes of this book and what we can learn from each profile examination, the conclusions can greatly enhance your leadership skills and how they can be applied in your career. Each chapter will draw conclusions about each leader; provide interpretive lessons for leaders; and offer some questions for reflection.

LEADERSHIP ATTRIBUTE MATRIX	
100 points for each category	
1. Integrity	00
2. Risk Taker	00
3. Communication	00
4. Passion	00
5. Vision	00
6. Resiliency	00
TOTAL SCORE for 00%	00
	600 points possible

Interpretative Lessons for Leaders

This section will be devoted to reflecting upon the profile of the specific leader and attempting to interpret lessons that you can learn as—the leader in your organization.

Aside from the compelling stories of the leaders profiled in this book, this section is the most important element in each profile. It encourages you to reflect upon their strengths and learn from what they did or how they achieved what they did. It is not about striving to be a prime minister, a king, or a queen. It is learning and understanding how they used their skills to achieve their results. At the end of each chapter, reflect upon what you have learned and how you might adapt or reinforce your leadership strengths to reach your goals, not only in your organization, but in your life.

Questions for Reflection

This section will offer three questions that will trigger a further discussion of the profiled leader.

References

Grofton, Ian. (2006). *The kings and queens of England.* London, England: Quercus Publishing PLC. p. 151.

Sears, Stephen W. (1994). *Lincoln and McClelellan in Lincoln's Generals*. Gabor S. Boritt. (Ed). New York: Oxford University Press. pp. 1-50.

The Civil War Society. (1997) *Civil war generals*. New York: Gramercy Books. pp. 27-30.

Neilson, William Allan and Charles Jarvis Hill (Eds) (1942). *The complete plays and poems of William Shakespeare*. Cambridge, Mass: The Riverside Press. pp. 734-735

Chapter 4
ALEXANDER THE GREAT

"My boy, you must find a kingdom big enough for your ambition. Macedonia is too small for you."[1]

Philip II, King of Macedonia

The Time Period

In order to fully understand the time in which Alexander the Great was born, it is important to know about the political situation and the military geography of that period. Alexander's father was Philip II, King of Macedonia, a land situated to the north of the Greek peninsula. At the birth of Alexander, Philip II had already

conquered large areas of Greece, which united the three most powerful city-states: Athens, Sparta, and Thebes, but they remained under Macedonian rule. These conquests brought an end to the period that is known as classical Greece. Philip II came to the throne at the early age of 24 and, during his reign, expanded the borders of Macedonia to include most of what we know as Greece. In addition, he reorganized his army; introduced new weaponry; and de-

---

[1] McCarty, p.18

vised new battle tactics. As a result, the Macedonian army was changed into a fearsome fighting machine.

Since Philip's ultimate ambition was to march his army into Asia, he formed the League of Corinth so that he could bring the entire Greek city-state power structure under a single banner. This became a uniting factor for Greece and became the basis for his move against the Persian Empire. He wanted to avenge Persia's attacks against Greece, which took place over the last one hundred years.

Alexander's mother was Olympias, a princess in her own right, who traced her lineage back to Achilles. Historians have said that she was a domineering mother and this, most certainly, would have affected Alexander. She also claimed that the Greek god, Zeus, was Alexander's spiritual father. Throughout Alexander's childhood, his mother frequently reminded him that he should act in a way that was always mindful of his heritage.

Alexander was born in the year 356 B.C. at the Macedonian capital of Pella. Upon the death of his father, King Philip, he became heir to the throne and the Macedonian empire that his father had acquired. The army was already well trained and armed with state of the art weaponry of the period. This was a huge advantage to Alexander as he began his public life as the new King of Macedonia.

Alexander's Early Life

In describing the influence that Alexander's mother and father had upon his early childhood and general psychological development, Fuller writes: "He inherited from her his passionate, mystical nature; from his father he inherited his energy and practical sense." [2] The royal life that Alexander was born into included the best tutors. As a young man, he was exposed to the arts and sciences. At the age of 14 years, Philip appointed Aristotle as his tutor and mentor. During the three years of his tutelage with Aristotle, Alexander developed a love of learning that did not diminish during his lifetime. Alexander was instructed in, not only philosophy, but in a wide range of the sciences. His instruction also included poetry and the *Iliad*. These are the influences that had an effect upon the man that he was to become.

There was a story told about Alexander that illustrates his courage and tenacity at a very young age. During those times, horse traders would often bring their horses into the king's presence so that they could show them off and possibly sell them to the King and his court. As the story is told, all the horses were sold with the exception of one exceptional stallion. The horse trader told the king that this stallion is fit for a king and only a person with strong hands can handle him. The horse trader offered Philip the stallion for 13 talents. Two of Phillip's advisors tried to mount the stallion and were quickly thrown off. At that point, the king said to the horse trader to take the stallion away and not bring him back. Alexander, overhearing this comment, asked his father if he could ride the horse. Alexander made a wager to his father that he could ride the horse, and if he did, his father would pay the 13 talents. Everyone, including his father who heard the wager, began to laugh. After a

---

[2] Fuller. p. 56

while, his father relented and reluctantly allowed Alexander an opportunity to mount the horse. With soft words to the horse and a slow and easy approach, Alexander vaulted onto the back of the stallion. Neither the horse nor the rider made any movement for a time. Then, the horse and rider bolted around and out of the pasture to the amazement of his father and all those who were observing. When he finally returned to the pasture where his father was waiting, everyone who witnessed what Alexander did that day, along with his father, broke out into applause for what they just saw him do. It was reported that his father said the following to his son: "My boy, you must find a kingdom big enough for your ambition. Macedonia is too small for you." [3] Alexander named his horse Bucephalus, which means "Ox Head." Bucephalus was with Alexander throughout most of his campaigns.

Alexander is Proclaimed King

At the age of 21, Alexander ascended to the throne after the assassination of his father. On the day of his father's death, Alexander was proclaimed King by the Macedonian army. They had already witnessed his courage at the earlier battle of Chaeronea where he commanded the left flank in support of King Philip's drive to the center of the opposing army. This was a milestone battle in the struggle to bring all of the Grecian city-states together under one ruler. His entire career was over a short 12 years later.

---

[3] McCarty p.18.

During his lifetime, he conquered most of the known world when most every other young man his age was still trying to find his place in life. His laser-like focus on learning the skills of the warrior; perfecting the strategy and tactics of combat; and experimenting with the skills of effectively administering a growing empire left him little time for any social endeavor.

Throughout his life, Alexander held an abiding love for his mother, Olympias. It was her strong influence and the many stories that she told him about his royal lineage and his connection to the god Zeus that he developed a kingly bearing that was less attributed to his throne, but more to his deep belief in his bloodline. He was both noble and chivalrous which were qualities rarely seen in a king at that time.

There was an incident which was recounted about Alexander's visit to the Oracle at Delphi. He had often reflected upon the stories of his heritage, which tended to reinforce his respect, not only for the spiritual realm, but also for other religions and cultures. He wanted to see what the prophecy would be for him and the kingdom that he inherited. At the insistence of Alexander, the priestess finally told him: "you are invincible, my son."[4] This statement, not only gave him courage and confidence, but led him to believe, at a deeper level, that he was god-like which led him to accept his semi-divine heritage.

There are many stories about how war was waged during that time period and the reader should not try to apply

---

[4] McCarty, p. 36.

contemporary standards of conduct and morality to a period of time in which war was conducted in a more brutal manner. The act of conquest, within its very definition, assumes that many lives would be lost. Aside from this impression of war during Alexander's time, he actually was a very compassionate man. This is a quality that some would see as unmanly or, in today's common vernacular, as not macho. However, Alexander was indeed his own man who chose his own path. It is written that he often exhibited chivalry toward women and enforced it with his armies. During the final battle against King Darius of Persia, he allowed the defeated King's wife and family to be treated with respect and instructed his army to continue to treat them as a royal family.

A story was told about Alexander when he and his army arrived in the Persian city of Gordium. A rope had been tied, a very long time ago, into a very complex knot that was referred to as the Gordian Knot. How to untie the knot was a puzzle that vexed many. It was said, that whoever the person that could untie the knot, would become the king of Asia. With his closest advisors watching what he would do, he experienced the stress of the moment. Alexander solved the problem in a most unusual way, which was consistent with his character. He took his sword from his scabbard and sliced the knot in two.

Commander & Leader

The defining battle that defeated King Darius and his Persian army was fought at Gaugamela in the year 331 BC. Although greatly outnumbered, Alexander's army won the day. In the years that followed, Alexander took his army into Egypt and eventually into India. Along the way, he adopted some of the customs and culture in the lands that he conquered. Through this process of gradual assimilation, Alexander made the people in those lands more compliant to his rule. It was Alexander's belief, and that of his father, that an empire must assimilate religions and cultures into one integrated rule in order for it to be sustained.

Alexander was fearless and his men knew it. He rode into battles with a white plume on his helmet, which marked him not only with his own army, but for the opposing army as a target. His constant demonstration of fearlessness and confidence developed courage and loyalty in his army that they wanted to be part of any battle and Alexander's eventual victories.

As a general, he listened to his men and heard their stories of battle. At the conclusion of a battle, he showed proper respect to the dying men in his army and also those in the opposing army. Honorable burials were given to those under his command who died and also to those who died opposing his army. When Alexander was in the field with his army, he shared all of their hardships. In a similar manner, when he acquired wealth as a result of his conquests, he shared the wealth with his army. Alexander was very good to his army by bestowing awards for performance and the designation of titles, which was part of the organizational structure of the army. These techniques helped to motivate his troops along with the fact that they wanted to be part of an army that won battles.

Alexander demonstrated a unique ability to organize and govern each of the conquered lands under the governorship called a *satrap*. Some of the lands that Alexander conquered had to be re-conquered due to weak management under his satraps. Although this system of organization kept his empire together and united under his leadership, it also contributed to its eventual breakup due to many weak *satraps* after his death.

By the time Alexander arrived in India, his army became more rebellious and wanted to return home. The army had been together for a number of years without an opportunity to step foot back in their homeland.

The man who had conquered the known world, died of a fever on June 10th in the year 323BC at the age of 32 years. When Alexander died, he had no plan in place for an heir to his empire. As a result, his generals fought among themselves and divided up his kingdom. All the lands, that had been united by Alexander into one enormous empire, were now lost.

Some Conclusions about This Leader

He was called Alexander the Great because he was a great leader of his army and the lands that he conquered. He led his army to victories while leading them from the front and confronting armies with far superior numbers. When he was in the field with his army, he shared their hardships, as well as, the wealth that was acquired from conquering other lands. He listened to the concerns of the soldiers and bestowed honors upon them with each victory that they brought to him.

His great vision for the lands that he conquered was to unite them under one ruler while adopting and diffusing their culture throughout his empire. He set up an organizational structure of regional satrap governors to manage his empire. Weak satraps caused parts of his empire to be reconquered. Unfortunately, this empire fell apart upon his death since he had made no vision for its eventual leadership.

Alexander's depth of self-confidence, courage, and extreme laser focus was underscored by a deep belief in his divine heritage, which reinforced his confidence in his leadership. He believed that he was invincible which enabled him to take great risks, but in taking those risks and achieving what he did, it caused his army to have a deep confidence in his leadership. Unfortunately, this depth of divine-inspired belief in himself was manifested, at times, in harm that he visited upon his closest friends. In a fit of rage, probably fueled by drink, he slew his closest friend. This outburst of emotion had a lasting impact on him for the rest of his life. These actions tended to peel away some of the integrity that his army held for him.

LEADERSHIP ATTRIBUTE MATRIX		
100 points for each category		
1. Integrity		80
2. Risk Taker		100
3. Communication		100
4. Passion		100
5. Vision		90
6. Resiliency		100
TOTAL SCORE for	95%	570
		600 points possible

Interpretative Lessons for Leaders

- A deep belief in yourself will enable you to do things you never thought possible. However, arrogance, toward those who follow you, could unravel all the good things that you do;

- Do not set yourself apart from those who you would lead. They know who you are and they know the rank in the organization that you hold;

- Listen to those who follow you. Acknowledge them and reward their achievements;

- Take risks in your life and in your career or you never will achieve anything of value;

- Leadership, without learning how to be a good manager, will cause you to fail;

- Cultures must be assimilated into one culture, if the organization is to be sustained.

Questions for Reflection

1) Weak satraps (governorships) forced Alexander to re-conquer parts of his empire. Is management a necessary skill of a leader or is it not necessary for a leader to manage? Explain.

2) Alexander exhibited extreme self-confidence that boarded upon arrogance. What is the difference between the two concepts? How would you go about building your self-confidence?

3) Alexander commanded a loyal army. Did you take note how he brought about this loyalty? How would you build a loyal team?

References

Adams, George Burton. (1919). *The rise of Macedonia and the conquests of alexander in European history: An outline of its development.* (pp. 42-51) London: The Macmillan Company.

Allen, John. (Ed.). (1945) *Alexander the Great in 100 Great lives.* (pp. 253-260). New York: The Greystone Press.

Bowra, C.M. (1965). *Alexander the great in Great ages of man: Classical Greece.* (pp. 157-165). New York: Time-Life Books.

Davis, Paul K. (Ed.) (1999). *Guagamela (Arbela) in 100 Decisive Battles: From ancient times to the present.* (pp. 31-34). New York: Oxford University Press.

Dupuy, Trevor N., Johnson, C., & Bongard, D. (1995). *Alexander III the Great in The Harper encyclopedia of military biography.* (pp. 27-28). Edison, New Jersey: Castle Books.

Fuller, J.F.C. (1960*). The generalship of Alexander the Great.* New Brunswick, New Jersey: Da Capo Press.

Hanson, Victor Davis. (Ed.) (2010). *Alexander the Great, nation building, and the creation and maintenance of empire in Makers of ancient strategy: From the Persian wars to the fall of Rome.* (pp. 118-137). Princeton, New Jersey: Princeton University Press.

Konstam, Angus. (2008). *Alexander the Great in Ancient world commanders: From the Trojan War to the fall of*

Rome. (pp. 25-30). London: Compendium Publishing Ltd.

McCarty, Nick. (2004). *Alexander the Great: The real life story of the world's greatest king.* (p. 18). New York: Carlton Publishing Group.

Roberts, Andrew. (Ed.) (2008). *Alexander the Great in The art of war: Great commanders of the ancient and medieval world 1500BC to 1600AD.* (pp. 124-131) London: Quercus.

Rodgers, Nigel. (2012) *Alexander the Great and his heirs in The illustrated encyclopedia of ancient Greece.* (pp. 132-252). Leicestershire, England: Lorenz Books.

Chapter 5
ELIZABETH I

*"I know that I have the body of a week
and feeble woman; but I have the heart
and stomach of a king"[1]*

Elizabeth I

At the age of 25, Elizabeth came to the throne of England in November of 1558 during a time of partisan religious chaos; a near bankrupt treasury; a weakened military after a conflict with France; and a languishing trade economy. During her 45-year reign as the Queen of England, many positive changes came to her country during this time period that is often referred to as the *Golden Age of England*. With the influence of the Italian Renaissance spreading across the European landscape, Elizabeth presided over a rebirth of her country into a leadership role as one of the most influential and powerful countries of the time. However, any reader who is familiar with the life of Elizabeth I would ask the question: how did she ever survive during the early years of her life, which included imprisonment

---

[1] Quercus. p. 25.

and multiple death threats, to become the Queen of England?

Elizabeth—the Child Princess

Let's begin the story of Elizabeth's life so that we can see how the events in those years affected her and how she acquired the resiliency of character that would serve her during her reign as Queen. Elizabeth was born in 1533 to King Henry VIII and Queen Anne Boleyn. She had a reddish-orange hair just like her father, so it was obvious that she was his child. Before she was 3 years old, her father had executed her mother on, what most historians believe, were trumped-up charges of infidelity. How this event affected her is really not known, but she did grow to love and admire her father.

As a young girl, Elizabeth was tutored in Greek, Latin, French, and Italian. She was considered to be well educated and intelligent. She developed a skill of being nimble and flexible as she navigated the politics and manners of the royal court. Her strength of will, coupled with a compassionate nature, afforded her the right balance of skills that she would eventually need in dealing with her ministers. These skills, along with her ability to be resilient, would serve her well during the reign of her sister Queen Mary and in her later years as Queen of England.

The Battle Over Religions

It is important to provide some historical context to the timeline in which Elizabeth grew up as a young child. During the reign of King Henry VIII, the royal houses of Europe believed in the divine right of kings. This belief placed Rome; the Catholic religion; and the Pope of Rome as the emissary of God, who officially blessed all of the royal houses of Europe. When King Henry VIII wanted to get a divorce from his wife Catherine of Aragon in order to wed Anne Boleyn, he sought an approval and a blessing from Pope Clement VII. When the Pope denied the King's request for divorce, King Henry VIII formed the Church of England; took the title of the Supreme Head of the Church of England; and wed Anne Boleyn. This was, essentially, the first time in centuries that any Royal House of Europe challenged the authority of the Pope of Rome. As a result of this defiance, the Pope excommunicated King Henry VIII from the Catholic Church. With this action, the English Reformation began. The Church of England, often referred to as the Protestant church, was the center of this reformation. The long-established culture of Roman Catholicism was being challenged by a new Protestant religion in which the King of England was the head of the church, not the Pope of Rome. Any English citizen, who failed to acknowledge the King of England as the Supreme Head of the Church of England, was persecuted and many were executed.

Anne Boleyn became the wife of King Henry and the Queen of England. Three years after their marriage and Anne's coronation as Queen, King Henry executed her on charges related to infidelity, which were never proven. The marriages of both Catherine of Aragon and Anne Boleyn were invalidated which had the effect of making Mary, the daughter of Catherine of Aragon, and Elizabeth, the daughter of Anne Boleyn, both illegitimate as it relates to the line of royal succession. Their half-brother, Edward, became the King of England upon the death of King Henry.

Edward VI became king of England at the age of nine years old. His reign only lasted six years as a result of poor health. At the age of 15, he died and, although he named Lady Jane Grey as his successor, Parliament reinstated the original royal line of succession approved by King Henry, which included both Mary and Elizabeth.

When Elizabeth's sister Mary ascended the throne, after the death of their brother Edward VI, she was determined to reinstate the Catholic religion as the official state religion of the realm. As the daughter of Catherine of Aragon, an ardent Catholic, she was raised with strong beliefs in the Catholic faith. With her marriage to Philip II of Spain, a Catholic monarch that was loyal to Rome, she became more determined than ever to reestablish the culture of Catholicism in England. Those who failed to openly practice the Catholic religion during the reign of Queen Mary were subject to the risk of imprisonment or death. There were many who were burned at the stake as heretics for not embracing the Catholic religion. It is for this reason that historians have often referred to her as "Bloody Mary".

Elizabeth favored the Protestant religion, which was the faith of her father. This choice put her at a grave risk during the reign of her sister Mary who was obsessed about bringing the English people back into Catholicism. Although there were a number of English factions who wanted Elizabeth on the throne since she was a Protestant, she always denied any association with these groups. This ongoing conflict between the Catholics and the Protestants put Elizabeth at great risk with her own sister. Her consistent professed loyalty to her sister, Queen Mary, brought about the opposite reaction from her own sister who imprisoned her in the Tower of London. One can only imagine the thoughts that might have run through Elizabeth's head during the time she was imprisoned in the Tower of London. She knew that her own mother was imprisoned in the Tower of London prior to her execution. Although she never served more than a few months in the Tower of London, she was under house arrest for almost a year.

Elizabeth Becomes Queen of England

Queen Mary died after a short reign of only five years. Elizabeth succeeded to the throne and was crowned Queen of England in 1558. Soon after her coronation, she established the Protestant church, which evolved into the Church of England, as we know it today. Although Elizabeth was not a Catholic, Pope Pius V excommunicated her. The Pope took one additional step and sent a message to the people of England that their Queen was illegitimate and the people of England did not need to obey her commands. The reign of Elizabeth I was more tolerant of Catholics then most would have expected. However, the Queen demanded loyalty from her subjects and outward expressions of the Catholic faith, especially the saying of the mass in public, drew swift punishment from the Queen. She steered a middle course for the ship of state in that she punished overt displays of practicing the Catholic faith, but did not attempt to question the religious beliefs of her subjects. It should be pointed out that during her reign as Queen, no heretic was burned at the stake for a religious belief. This policy brought an end to religious persecution in England.

Elizabeth loved her subjects and she loved England. There are many accounts of her visiting various parts of her realm to meet and talk with her subjects. During these times and during multiple addresses to the Parliament, she displayed her exemplary skills for compassion, communication, and public speaking. Parliament consistently badgered the Queen to take a husband since the line of succession to the throne was of paramount importance. Since Elizabeth had dozens of suitors, her exceptional communication skills helped her to hold them and Parliament at bay and, thereby, maintain a balance of peace in England until it became apparent that to all that she was married to England. Historians would eventually refer to her as the "virgin" Queen.

One of the significant events that occurred during the reign of Elizabeth was the execution of her cousin, Mary Queen of Scots. It is critical to this story to explain the context around the events that led to her execution. In the eyes of the Pope and the Catholic Church, Mary Queen of Scots, an ardent catholic, was recognized as the lawful and legitimate queen of England. Mary was the granddaughter of Henry VII and the daughter of Margaret who was the wife of James IV of Scotland. Amidst the intense rivalries of the nobles in Scotland and the palace intrigues surrounding the death of her husband, Mary fled to England to seek the protection of her cousin, Elizabeth. In essence, Mary was a Queen without a country.

Soon after her arrival in England, the Catholic factions began to plot ways to put her on the throne of England. There were multiple death threats against Elizabeth during this time. One of the conspiracies, known as the Babington plot, was discovered which strongly implicated Mary. Although Mary was tried and convicted, Elizabeth found it very difficult to sign the execution order for her own cousin. After some reflection, Elizabeth realized that the plots and conspiracies, against her life, would continue unless Mary was executed. Elizabeth reluctantly signed the order from Parliament and Mary, Queen of Scots, was executed in 1587.

The defeat of the Spanish Armada in 1588 was an historic turning point in the fortunes of both Spain and England. Philip II, an ardent Catholic, had been married to Mary, sister of Queen Elizabeth, until her death in 1558. His hatred of the Protestants and Elizabeth's execution of Mary Queen of Scots caused the relationship between the two countries to sever. The final insult that caused Spain to go to war with England was the fact that English privateers were capturing Spanish ships and taking their precious cargos.

Elizabeth Leads her Country

Prior to the battle, Sir Francis Drake, an English privateer, raided a number of ports along the Spanish coast that caused severe damage to both their ships and supplies. The actual battle pitted 130 large Spanish vessels against 197 small and maneuverable English vessels. The smaller and more maneuverable English vessels and the experience of their crews gave the advantage to the English captains during this engagement. It should be understood that Spain's sea power was the strongest in the known world at this time. After the Spain sent an enormous Armada of ships for the English Channel, they unexpectedly had to bring their boats to a port in order to avoid an unexpected storm at sea. While the Armada was anchored at a port, the English captains set a number of their small ships on fire and sent them toward the anchored Spanish fleet. Many of the large Spanish vessels were set ablaze and it was not long before the Spanish fleet turned around and headed back towards Spain. Just prior to this battle, Elizabeth I rode out to rally her troops with the following speech:

> I know I have the body of a weak and feeble woman, but I have a heart and stomach of a king, and a king of England too, and I think foul scorn that Parma or Spain or any prince of Europe should dare to invade the borders of my realm; to which, rather than any dishonour shall grow by me, I myself will take up arms, I myself will be your general, judge and rewarder of everyone of your virtues in the field.[2]

The policies of Elizabeth allowed England to experience a renaissance of the arts, including the literary work of William Shakespeare. With the defeat of the Spanish Armada, England grew to become one of the strongest naval

---

[2] Crofton. p. 151.

powers in the world, which ultimately led to the English colonization of North America. The command of the seas allowed England to build up their treasury by increasing trade from all parts of the world.

Some Conclusions about This Leader

Elizabeth was not quite three years old when her father put her mother, Queen Anne Boleyn, to death. It must have been very difficult for a young girl of that age to understand why her mother was taken away from her. As she grew up, she learned that she must be very discreet about what she says and about the opinions she expressed. This early understanding in her life was probably the single reason why she survived to become queen of England. Some authors have expressed the point of view that Elizabeth was indecisive as a queen. However, a number of other authors, including myself, believe that if she expressed an early opinion on an issue it could have major consequences for herself, as well as, for England. So, what some may have perceived as indecisive, others saw as strategic thinking.

In a further reflection on her life, Elizabeth loved her subjects and they loved her. Often during her reign as queen, she would visit her people throughout the realm. Her skill in communication and public speaking, in addition to the quality of compassion, helped her to win the hearts of her people.

One of the things that she did early in her reign as Queen was to put forth a temperate and more measured policy of toleration for those who professed the Catholic faith.

Since the Protestant church had become the official religion of England, it is understandable why she needed to enforce her laws and policy around the outward profession of the Catholic faith. However, it speaks well for Elizabeth's reign that she was temperate about its enforcement. In other words, she did not want to prosecute people because of their beliefs.

Just prior to the attack and eventual failure of the Spanish Armada in 1588, Elizabeth I, Queen of England, rode out to meet her troops and let them know that she was one of them. She told them that she was their general and that she would suffer the same fate as they would. She also said that she would reward those who fought valiantly in the field.

It was her leadership, against a far superior force at this pivotal point in history, that marked the downward spiral of Spain's command of the seas and the growth of English dominance in the world's oceans. This event in history opened the door to English colonization of North America and the eventual establishment of the United States of America.

LEADERSHIP ATTRIBUTE MATRIX	
100 points for each category	
1. Integrity	100
2. Risk Taker	70
3. Communication	100
4. Passion	100
5. Vision	80
6. Resiliency	100
TOTAL SCORE for	92% 550
	600 points possible

Interpretative Lessons for Leaders

- Express support and loyalty to your boss. You will set the example for others to follow when you are the boss;

- Take time to get to know those who follow you. Be authentic in your leadership and by doing so, you will create a loyal following;

- Understand that you will sometimes be confronted with polarized issues that may be difficult to choose one side or the other. Find middle ground and work with your followers to understand how to navigate the new norm.

- Lead from the front and take calculated risks

Questions for Reflection

1) What did you learn from Queen Elizabeth's silence
   while under the rule of her sister, Queen Mary? How
   important is it to speak your mind all the time? Explain.

2) When Elizabeth rode with her army to meet the Spanish
   Armada, she led from the front. When was the last time
   that you led from the front with your team? Elaborate.

3) How did Queen Elizabeth engender loyalty from her
   subjects? What actions would you take to build loyalty
   from your workforce?

References

Allen, John. (1945) *Queen Elizabeth in 100 great lives.* (pp. 163-168). New York: The Greystone Press.

Andrews, Charles M. (1912). *The age of Elizabeth: England becomes a protestant power of the first rank in a short history of England* (pp. 217-249). Boston: Allyn and Bacon.

Canning, John. (Ed.). (1985). *Queen Elizabeth I in 100 great kings, queens, and rulers of the world* (pp. 438-443). New York: Hamlyn Publishing Group Ltd.

Cawthorne, Nigel. (2009). *The tudors in the kings and queens of England.* (pp. 92-119) New York: Arcturus Publishing Limited.

Crofton, Ian. (2006). *Elizabeth I in The kings and queens of England.* (pp. 145-153). London: Quercus Publishing.

Davis, Paul K. (Ed.). (1999). *Spanish armada in 100 decisive battles from ancient times to the present.* (pp. 199-204). Oxford: Oxford University Press.

Green, John Richard. (1886). *The England of Elizabeth 1558-1561 in History of the English people.* (Vol 2, pp. 202-234). New York: WM. L. Allison.

Haigh, Christopher. (1988) *Profiles in power Elizabeth I.* New York: Longman Group.

Longford, Elizabeth, (Ed.). *Elizabeth I in The oxford book of royal anecdotes.* (pp. 232-246). Oxford: Oxford University Press.

Lord, John (1885). *Queen Elizabeth in beacon lights of history*. (pp. 223-264). New York: Fords, Howard, and Hulbert.

Perry, Maria. (1990). *The word of a prince.* Suffolk, England: The Boydell Press.Quercus Publishing. (2005) (p. 25). New York.

Matthews, George T., (Ed.). (1959). *News and rumor in renaissance Europe the fugger newsletters*, New York: Capricon Books.

Chapter 6
PETER THE GREAT

"Never have the collected qualities of a nation, good and bad, been so summed up in a single personality, destined to be its historic type... Peter is Russia—her flesh and blood, her temperament, her virtues and her vices."[1]

Kazimierz Waliszewski
An author of Russian history

Barbarism in Russia

The early history of Russia was marked by a significant Asian influence from the east. Russia's evolving culture was further marked by a conquest brought about by the Mongol army of Genghis Khan and the barbaric and nomadic tribes that settled in Russia in the 13th century. This level of barbarism set Russia apart from the civilizing influence of Western Eur-  ope. An isolationist culture grew from these influences and inhibited the modernization of Russian organizations and systems. Over the next four centuries, Russia embraced Catholic Christianity and evolved into a more homogeneous society, but maintained its rural and agrarian social or-

---

[1] Johnston. (1924) p. 179

der. By the 17th century, Russia was considered as a weak
military power among the family of Euro-Asian countries
due to the lack of a disciplined army and the absence of a
navy. This was the cultural landscape of Russia when Peter
became the Czar of Russia.

Early Influences

Peter was born on June 9, 1672 to Czar Alexis and his
second wife, Natalya Naryshkina, as their first child. When
Peter was four years old, Czar Alexis died and Theodore, or
Feodor as he was often called, was the elder half-brother
and godfather to Peter who succeeded to the throne. During
the next several years, Peter was tutored and exposed to
learning multiple languages, history, and events that shaped
his world at that time. He read the Bible and memorized
large passages of the Bible, as was customary. His mother
noticed his love of learning so she arranged for the national
library to create a number of books, with many pictures, for
him to see and to read. As a result of this special concern of
his mother, he developed a special interest in military and
naval history. As the godson to the ruling Czar, Peter was
afforded every opportunity to increase his learning and
widen his education. These early years had a great influence upon him and provided a focus for what he accomplished in his later life.

When Peter was 10 years old, his godfather and Czar
Theodore (Feodor) died. Although Peter was proclaimed
Czar, the event triggered a revolution. The claims to succession by his half-brother Ivan were ignored until their
sister Sophia triggered a revolt. It is interesting to note that
some historians have described Ivan as dull-witted. The is-

suc of succession was eventually resolved in favor of a co-ruler model by both Ivan and Peter with their sister Sophia as Regent.

During the next 14 years while Sophia ruled as Regent, internal conflicts with the nobles, both inside and outside Moscow, continued and many people were tortured and killed. Although Peter grew up as a Czar while his sister ruled Russia, he and his mother retreated to the countryside. It was there that the young teenage Peter played war games with his friends and became fascinated with all things military. He created real regiments that were supported with horses, supply wagons, and artillery.

Peter Rules Russia with his Brother

It was in the year 1696, upon the death of his brother and co-ruler Ivan, that Peter was proclaimed Sovereign of all of Russia at the age of 24. His sister, Sophia who was now quite comfortable as a ruler, engineered a failed coup to topple Peter from his place as Czar. Peter discovered the plot and exiled or executed her supporters while sending her off to a convent. This was the first of many attempts on Peter's life.

As a young man, Peter grew in physical strength and to a height of almost 7 feet tall. His earlier childhood fascination with all things military became the focus of his later life, which eventually led to the westernization of Russia and the complete reorganization of Russian government and administrative systems as a direct result of his many reforms.

When Peter arrived at the Kremlin, the center of government in Russia, he discovered that most ministers and administrative staff had acquired their position through political favoritism and not through their own talents and qualifications. The court nobles were fighting amongst themselves for a coveted limited number of positions in the government. The chaos that he found in the Kremlin was representative of what existed throughout the military. Russia's small army was undisciplined, inexperienced, and lacking the necessary skills and strategic knowledge of warfare.

One of the first things that Peter did was to appoint new ministers and government officials who were loyal to him and possessed the experience and qualifications for the positions that they held. Although he heard about western European skills such as carpentry, shipbuilding, general military and warfare skills, he had no first-hand knowledge of these skills nor had he ever visited Western Europe. In the year 1697, Peter sent 19 noblemen to Venice to learn about contemporary warfare skills along with a letter of introduction to the Doge. He also sent many other Russians to European countries in order to learn skills that could be brought back to Russia in order to train others.

The Czar Becomes a Dock Worker

In that same year, Peter made his first visit to a Western European country when he visited Holland. The purpose of the visit was to learn carpentry and other shipbuilding skills since boats had always fascinated Peter. However, the Czar disguised himself as a poor dockworker in order to learn the skills of shipbuilding. He wasn't afraid of hard work and he felt that he would not learn the skills if he had introduced himself as the Czar of Russia. It was not long before the people in the area heard about the Czar disguised as a dockworker and wanted to see him. Peter was not afraid of hard work and he was known to have calluses on his hands from the work that he performed. He possessed a great deal of energy throughout his life and, although he was the Czar of Russia, he was always engaged in learning some new trade. During the same period of time, Peter also visited England in an effort to learn more about naval architecture.

During the reign of Czar Peter the Great, Russia was exposed to three threats on its borders: Turkey to the south; Sweden to the north; and France to the west. Russia was essentially a land locked country with no access to the sea. Peter reasoned that unless Russia was able to gain an access to the sea, it would continue to be at a disadvantage for commerce, trade, and defense. He decided to build a strong navy and reorganized his army so that they understood the strategy and tactics of warfare.

Commercial Access to the Black Sea

After several battles with turkey, Peter acquired Russian access to the Black Sea. During the early 18th century, Sweden was considered to be one of the greatest military powers in Europe and it controlled access to the Baltic Sea. By this time, Peter had strengthened his army sufficiently to defeat Sweden in the battle at Poltava in 1709, which gave Russia, for the first time, access to the Baltic Sea. It also dethroned Sweden as the premier military power at that time. Shortly thereafter, in the year 1712, Peter established a major seaport on the Baltic and built the city of St. Petersburg, which became the new capital of Russia.

Throughout Peter's reign as the Czar of Russia, he was constantly seeking new sources of revenue to support his growing and reorganized mílitary. He introduced new sources of revenue, but at the same time, he wanted to impose a sense of fairness in the process. He reduced the privileges of the nobles in favor of acquiring higher levels of expertise that would help grow the country's industry. He offered incentives to those Russians who were willing to travel to Europe and learn new skills that could be imported back into Russian society. He favored those who were willing to join the military and reduced or eliminated their tax obligations.

One Russian Culture

Peter recognized that one of the internal threats to Russia was its multi-faceted and disparate culture that was constantly at war with itself. He wanted to change the political landscape so that all Russians would come together as one country, rather than a country of warring tribes. All of the reforms that Peter brought to Russia were imposed by force since that was the only way that change could have occurred at this time in Russia's history.

Many of these reforms did not sit well with the nobles and, as a consequence, Peter was constantly overseeing his own directives in order to ensure compliance with his policies and reduce some of the corruption that leaked into their administration. As the influence and power of the nobles was reduced, the task of ensuring compliance was made more difficult. Peter's numerous reforms brought back from Europe contemporary ideas in shipbuilding, warfare, and the tools to increase trade for his country. There was a great deal of opposition with many powerful groups within Russia to the westernization of their country. However, Peter did not seek to westernize Russia, but simply bring it out of its isolation into the Euro-Asian family of countries by using contemporary methods and tools.

During his reign as Czar (1682-1725), Peter introduced new principles of administration; town councils with elected representatives; and a number of colleges of learning that inspired the continued growth of its people and its administrative systems. He also opened up Russia to the Renaissance that had already swept across Europe. Peter the Great, as he was later to be called, accomplished a great deal in the short time during his reign as Czar. He changed institutions and brought a barbaric society into the civilized family of European nations.

Some Conclusions about This Leader

Some say that Peter was more suited to become a carpenter or a naval architect, but not a Czar of Russia. When he was young, he did not learn of politics and political court intrigue, but rather he played war with his friends. Peter was shy and considered an introvert. He acquired a deep sense of the love of learning and developed a fascination for all things military. His obsession with all things military led him to find new sources of revenue to support the building of his Navy and the reorganization of his army. It was during this phase of his reign, that he realized that he must reorganize and restructure the administrative systems that brought revenue into Russia. His fascination with Western Europe eventually led him to open the doors of Russia to the civilized part of the larger family of nations.

The most significant reforms that Peter brought to Russia included education and commerce. The reforms that he brought to Russia, far too numerous to mention here, were implemented through the force of his will and against the multiple power brokers that existed throughout his country. Simply directing that these forms be instituted would have been insufficient to put them into place. He was forced to constantly manage the implementation of his directives or the reforms would never have happened.

LEADERSHIP ATTRIBUTE MATRIX 100 points for each category	
1. Integrity	80
2. Risk Taker	100
3. Communication	60
4. Passion	100
5. Vision	100
6. Resiliency	90
TOTAL SCORE for 88%	530
	600 points possible

Interpretative Lessons for Leaders

• Leaders must quickly size up a situation before it gets out of control. When Peter came to the throne, he had to act quickly or he would have been assassinated;

- Leadership and management are two sides of the same coin. Every leader must manage, as well as, lead. A leader who fails to manage may end up losing everything;

- A leader must become a lifelong learner. It is through learning that new ideas and concepts become crystalized. Peter learned from the western European countries and brought back into Russia new ideas, tools, and an entire renaissance of learning;

- Put into place systems that will include people who are qualified to manage for you. Be fair and inclusive in their selection.

- Be humble, but assertive. Don't fall in love with your own power and influence.

Questions for Reflection

1) Why must you always manage the manager? What did you learn from Peter's overseeing his managers? Discuss

2) As you read the profile for Peter the Great, you could discern that he had a grand vision for his country. What was his grand vision and what is your grand vision for your organization?

3) What is the stronger characteristic of essential leadership: Fear or Motivation? What element did Peter use? What would you use? Provide an opinion and defend.

References

Adams, George Burton. (1919). *The rise of Russia and Prussia in European history*. (pp. 386-392) New York: The Macmillan Company.

Allen, John. (1945) *Peter the Great in 100 Great lives*. (pp. 369-376) The Greystone Press. New York.

Bushkovitch, Paul. (2001). *Peter the great*. Lanham, MD.: Rowman & Littlefield Publishers, Inc.

Davis, Paul K. (Ed.). (1999). *Poltava in 100 decisive battles from ancient times to the present*. (pp. 231-236). Oxford: Oxford University Press.

Dupuy, Trevor N., Johnson, C., & Bongard, D. (1995). *Peter I the great in The Harper encyclopedia of military biography*. (pp. 589-590). Edison, New Jersey: Castle Books.

Johnston, John T. (1924). *Peter the great in world patriots*. (pp. 177-187). Saint Louis, USA: World Patriots Company.

Klyuchevsky, Vasli. (1958). *Peter the great*. Boston. Beacon Press.

Mander, Samuel. (1854). *The history of Russia in The history of the world*. (pp. 199-214). New York: Henry Bill.

Wale, William. (1902). *What great men have said about great men*. (p. 315). London: Swan Sonnenschein & Co.

Williamson, Geoffrey. (1985) *Peter I (The Great) in 100 great kings, queens, and rulers of the world* in J. Canning (Ed.). (pp. 484-489). New York: Hamlyn Publishing Group Ltd.

Chapter 7

GEORGE WASHINGTON
Commander & Founding Father of a Country

"England missed the sobriety, the self-command, the perfect soundness of judgment, the perfect rectitude of intention, to which the history of revolutions furnishes no parallel, or furnishes a parallel in Washington alone.[1]"

John Hampden Wale

George Washington was at the epicenter of a contest of wills between the greatest naval power of the 18th-century and a fledgling colony in North America. This battle of wills also had an affect on another major European country and was a contributing factor in its landmark revolution for independence. Of course, I am referring to the American Revolution and their battle with the British Empire in the 18th century. The major European country, to which I refer, is France who provided military and financial assistance to the colonists in their fight for independence, but increased their debt to the point where it became a ma-

---

[1] Wale, p. 453.

jor contributing factor that ignited the French Revolution of 1789.

What were the factors, which placed George Washington in this pivotal chain of events and put him into a position to lead his country to victory over England and assume the honored title of: Father of his Country? What leadership qualities did he possess that gave him the skills and abilities to win a battle against the greatest naval power at that time? We will explore these questions and more as we profile the life of George Washington.

Early Influences

George Washington was born on February 22nd in the year 1732 to Augustine and Mary Ball Washington. Augustine was a shrewd business owner who acquired land, situated along the Potomac River, as well as, some land located beside Pope's Creek near the small town of Fredericksburg in Virginia. The Washington family chose to make their home at this Pope's Creek site. Although much of his property was inherited, Augustine's multiple business enterprises augmented his considerable holdings. Due to Augustine's early death, Mary became a strong influence to George as he was growing into a young man. She was a strong willed woman who displayed an uncompromising and stubborn independence, which can also be seen as a personality trait in her son. Throughout his life, there existed a rather contentious relationship between George and his mother, which engendered an occasional internal rage. George kept this rage in check by presenting an outwardly stoic demeanor. As a result, he was observed by many of his peers to be a quiet and serious-minded man who exhibited occasional bouts of temper.

Although the Washington's were not considered wealthy at that time, their income was generated by the sale of tobacco from their vast fields; other business interests; and their slave labor. They lived in the colonies established by and under the protection of the British Empire and George II, King of England. Although all commerce was controlled by England, it was a period of time of peace and relative contentment as the wealth and prosperity of the colonies flourished.

George had two older brothers who were sent off by their father to England to obtain a formal education. George, of course, expected to receive a similar education, but it was unavailable to him as result of the untimely death of his father. The lack of a formal education really affected George and his self-confidence for the rest of his life. When George's father died, he turned to his older brother, Lawrence, as his mentor and advisor.

Washington Becomes a Colonial Officer

In 1739 a conflict broke out between England and Spain over an incident in the Caribbean. Lawrence accepted a commission as a colonial captain in the British Navy and served in that conflict. As a result of his military experience, Lawrence was named as an Adjutant General for the colony of Virginia. He was given a royal commission with the rank of major and charged with building a militia in Virginia. It was this event that first made George

Washington aware of the significant differences between a colonial commission and the royal commission. The royal commission was indeed more prestigious since it originated from the King of England while the colonial commission was simply an officer in a support of colonial role. Eventually, George Washington's ambition would cause him to follow in the footsteps of his brother and become an Adjutant General for Virginia in the colonial military and rise to the rank of colonel. Although he desperately coveted a royal commission during the entire time he served in the British colonial forces, it was denied to him on multiple occasions. There is a bit of irony here. If he had obtained a royal commission, would George Washington have ever commanded the American forces in the American Revolution and become the Father of his Country?

In order to understand how George Washington was selected as the commander of the American colonial forces during the American Revolution, we must digress to understand the historical relationship between the French and the English. The French and Indian War (1754-1763) was the final conflict in a larger war, which lasted 100 years between these two major European powers over colonization in North America. When the French began to encroach into the Ohio Valley, England realized that they must prevent further colonization. Governor Robert Dinwiddie, the King's representtative in Virginia, directed 21-year-old Washington and seven others to go into the Ohio Valley and assess the strength of the French forces. Upon meeting the French commander, Washington was warned that any attempt at English colonization in the Ohio Valley would be met with resistance.

The Colonel Starts a War

After reporting this news to Governor Dinwiddie, Washington was directed to return to the valley with an advance detachment of 120 men. Along the way, he encountered a friendly Indian chief with a dozen braves. When the Indian Chief informed him that there was a nearby French encampment, Washington set out with 40 soldiers, and the Indians, to meet the French. After traveling 6 miles, the French encampment was discovered. Colonel Washington directed his men to surround the encampment and then gave the signal to attack. Ten French soldiers were killed and 31 were captured in the attack. This event became the battle that triggered the start of the French and Indian War in 1754. This blunder weighed heavily on Washington for years. "While the folks at home embraced him as an improbable hero, Washington was denigrated in England as a reckless young warrior and in France as an outright assassin."[2]

As the war grew into years, Colonel Washington distinguished himself, on several occasions, through the demonstration of his courage; his ability to lead; and his integrity. These qualities, along with his knowledge of the strengths and weaknesses of the English; their battle tactics; and experience in frontier fighting elevated his reputation with the American colonists and eventually led to his selection as their commander-in- chief in the war for Independence. When the French and Indian War concluded in 1763 with the Treaty of Paris, George Washington had estab-

---

[2] Chernow, p. 45.

lished a military reputation that was greater than any other leader in the colonies. This was a pivotal period for George Washington, which was to soon launch him into greatness.

In 1759, while the French and Indian War was being waged, George met and married a wealthy widow by the name of Martha Dandridge Custis. They made their home on property situated along the Potomac River, which George inherited shortly after the death of his brother Lawrence. By that time, this property was known as Mount Vernon. The property was so named by Lawrence in memory of a favorite British admiral that he had served with in the Royal Navy.

Planter and Farmer

For the next 15 years, George Washington settled into the role of a planter, a farmer, and a politician. While enjoying his new roles, he developed an obsession with always wearing the proper attire. With his exposure to English culture and manners, he wanted to be accepted on his terms and be seen as an elegant gentleman. Standing over 6 feet tall, George Washington had reddish brown hair and never wore an English white wig. He was not an accomplished orator, probably due to his lack of self-confidence about his limited education and the troublesome false teeth that plagued him most of his life. As his recognition and acclaim grew, he began to become aware of his place in history.

The period of peace and relative contentment, as a colony of the British Empire, was soon coming to a close.

King George II had died and King George III succeeded him in 1760. England's House of Commons and the King decided to levy a tax (Stamp Act 1765) against the American colonies in an effort to force them to bear a part of the long and expensive war with France. Other taxes soon followed. As a leading planter and politician in the American colonies, George Washington and other colonial leaders began to feel the sting of British taxation. "… Washington emerged as a significant political leader a full year before being named to head the Continental Army, no fence-sitter, this conservative planner was a true militant."[3] The colonial resistance led to the establishment of the Continental Congress in 1774 and eventually the appointment of General George Washington in 1775, as commander-in-chief of the Continental Army.

Commander-in-Chief

One of the monumental challenges confronting General Washington during the entire Revolutionary War was all about military resources. With enlistments constantly expiring, there was an inevitable turnover of experienced fighting men and the need to train the new recruits. He had to find a way to increase the size and strength of his army. In 1775, General Washington requested and Congress approved to allow slaves to enlist voluntarily in the Army. Blacks made up 6-12% of the Continental Army.[4] Another huge resource challenge was to get the thirteen colonies to

---

[3] Chernow, p. 168.
[4] Chernow, p. 213.

pay their fair share of expenses associated with food, clothing, and military ordinance supplies for the army. The lack
of these resources caused undue hardship and death at their
winter encampments, including Valley Forge. Washington
was always looking after the needs of his Army. One
Frenchman had this to say about Washington: "I could not
keep my eyes from that imposing countenance: grave yet
not severe; affable without familiarity. Its predominant
expression was calm dignity, to which you can trace the
strong feelings of the patriot and discern the father as well
as the commander of his soldiers."[5]

Washington and his generals fought a war with the
English using frontier fighting methods while employing
the elements of deception, whenever possible, to outwit
their enemy. Washington used his spy network and the
communications techniques of the day to deceive the enemy. On several occasions, Washington moved his fighting
forces stealthily away from a greatly superior English force
usually during the dead of night. He kept their campfires
burning; used hay bales to screen movements; and covered
wagon wheels to reduce the sound of movement. He was
often seen on the battlefield leading his men astride his
horse while risking his own life.

On Christmas Eve 1776, Washington met with his
generals to plan the crossing of the Delaware River on
Christmas Day to surprise the Hessian garrison at Trenton.
One of the characteristics of Washington was his ability to
listen intently to his general staff before he made a final
decision, after thinking it through. Once made, it was

---

[5] Chernow, p. 326

nearly impossible to change his mind. Washington knew that if he were captured, the war would be over. Nevertheless, he believed in never asking his men to do anything in which he would not also share the risk. As they crossed the ice-encrusted river with his force of 2,400, they encountered a severe storm and buffeting winds that increased the possibility of failure. The Hessians, not only believed that the Americans would not try to cross the Delaware in the dead of winter, they also believed that the Americans would not dare go up against the professional Hessian soldiers. The victory for the Continental Army at Trenton was complete. There were 22 Hessians killed; 84 wounded; and nearly 900 were captured; while only two Americans were killed. It was highly probable that this singular victory helped to convince the French to lend the fledging colonies soldiers and monetary assistance.

Although Washington lost many battles in the Revolutionary War, he never surrendered and he kept his army together which was a real feat of leadership. With the final victory at Yorktown in 1781, Washington was eager to return to his beloved Mount Vernon. Little did he realize that his new country still had a need for his leadership.

First President of the United States

In 1787, the Continental Congress came together in Philadelphia for the purpose of strengthening the original articles of Confederation. However, behind closed doors, and with the utmost secrecy, a new Constitution was drafted. Without George Washington's presence and participation at this historic event, it might not have happened at all. The reputation and popularity of Washington among the colonies, in effect, legitimized the entire event.

After the final ratification of the new constitution in 1789, George Washington was unanimously elected the country's first new president. One of the most significant issues that he took upon himself, as the new president, was to establish a national bank; implement an effective tax system; and pay off all of the national and state debts related to the war. He and Alexander Hamilton, his Treasury Secretary, believed that other countries would see these actions as responsible and, thereby, it would encourage commerce and good faith credit among trading nations. If these financial systems had been in existence during the war, Washington would have had the necessary resources to purchase food, clothing, pay his soldiers, and obtain military ordinance to more quickly win the war.

George Washington served two terms as president and then retired to Mount Vernon in 1797. Two years later, he died in 1799 at the age of 67. He had given much of his life to his country.

Some Conclusions about This Leader

As George Washington grew into a young man and, finally a colonial soldier of England, he was greatly influenced by his brother Lawrence and came to emulate and identify with the culture and the customs of England. Although he coveted a royal commission in England's military, he was denied this prize on multiple occasions. Throughout his career as a soldier, he created and wore a fashionable blue military tunic that was similar to Britain's Royal red tunic worn by the English soldier. He was always impeccably dressed and believed that it was a requirement of a gentleman. The absence of a formal education weighed heavily upon him throughout his career and affected the self-confidence he had in conversing with others and in public speaking. As a result of this, he compensated by developing a habit of asking many questions to thoroughly understand the issue being discussed.

Although he desired public acclaim for his accomplishments, since he was a very ambitious man, he never sought it publically. He always managed to have others speak about his accomplishments, which had the effect of increasing his reputation. He made the biggest blunder that any soldier could make and that was—he started the French and Indian war as a result of poor judgment. Although he was only 21 years old at the time, he learned from it and became more cautious in making decisions. He was known to tentatively listen to his staff; weigh the arguments, and plumb the depths of the issue before making a final decision. Once it was made, he rarely changed it.

"Washington's inestimable strength, whether as a general, a planter, or a politician, was prolonged deliberation and slow, mature decisions, but these were luxuries seldom permitted in the heat and confusion of battle."[6] General Washington lost many more battles than he won, but he found a way to keep his army together and fight using a frontier style of hit and run that worked for him.

---

[6] Chernow, p. 306.

As a result of the lessons he learned as a general, he was able to bring them into the Presidency, which helped to frame the new constitution of this infant nation.

LEADERSHIP ATTRIBUTE MATRIX	
100 points for each category	
1. Integrity	90
2. Risk Taker	100
3. Communication	50
4. Passion	100
5. Vision	100
6. Resiliency	100
TOTAL SCORE for 90%	540
	600 points possible

Interpretative Lessons for Leaders

• Get as much education as you can. It will give you the tools to grow in your career, but it will also give you a strong sense of self-confidence;

• Just because you might have a failure early in your career, it is what you do next that makes the difference. Don't let one mistake define who you are;

- Dress the part of your workplace. Adopt the attire of those who you want to be like;

- Carefully consider all aspects of a problem and listen to your staff before making a final decision. There is always at least two points of view to every problem;

- Never allow yourself to proclaim your own accomplishments, but allow others to do so. Make yourself visible to your particular community of interest and it will happen.

Questions for Reflection

1) Is it important for a leader to lead from the front? Why? How did Washington lead from the front?

2) Aside from resumes and vitas, how can a leader let people, in positions of authority, know about their special skills and achievements? How did Washington build his reputation? How would you build your reputation?

3) Is there a relationship between academic achievements and on-the-job accomplishments? What did you learn from Washington's profile about this issue?

References

Chernow, Ron. (2010). Washington: a life. New York: the Penguin Group.

Crofton, Ian. (2006). George III in The kings and queens of England. (pp. 199-204). London: Quercus Publishing.

Davis, Paul K. (Ed.) (1999). Trenton, Saratoga, and Yorktown in 100 Decisive Battles: From ancient times to the present. (pp. 248-263). New York: Oxford University Press.

Dupuy, Trevor N., Johnson, C., & Bongard, D. (1995). *George Washington in The Harper encyclopedia of military biography.* (pp. 785-786). Edison, New Jersey: Castle Books.

Founding of the United States. (2014). England: Imagine Publishing LTD.

Henriques, Peter R. (2006). *Realistic visionary: a portrait of George Washington.* Charlottesville: University of Virginia Press.

Larson, Edward J. (2014). *The return of George Washington 1783-1789.* New York: HarperCollins Publishers.

Paine, Thomas. (1776). *Common sense.* Republished New York: Barnes & Noble

Raphael, Ray. (2004). *Founding myths: stories that hide our patriotic past.* New York: The New Press

Russell, Francis. (1962). *The French and Indian wars.* New York: American Heritage Publishing Co., Inc.

Wale, William. (1902). *What great men have said about great men.* (p. 453). London: Swan Sonnenschein & Co.

Chapter 8

WINSTON CHURCHILL, the Statesman

"We shall not flag or fail. We shall fight in France, we shall fight on the seas and oceans, we shall fight with growing confidence and growing strength in the air, we shall defend our island, whatever the cost may be, we shall fight on the beaches, we shall fight on the landing grounds, we shall fight in the fields and in the streets, we shall fight in the hills. We shall never surrender."[1]

Winston Churchill
Prime Minister of England

Winston Churchill was very popular with the English people yet, at the same time, he was despised and belittled by his own colleagues in Parliament as a warmonger. Prior to 1933 when Adolf Hitler came to power in Germany as it's Chancellor, Churchill warned the English people that Germany was growing in military strength and that England should begin rearmament for it's own self-protection. The Parliament did not want to hear anything about rearmament since the country was trying to recover from the effects of

---

[1] Johnson. (2009). p. 116.

World War I and the Great Depression of 1929, which led to a 10-year economic event. The last thing that the British people wanted to hear was the possibility of war becoming to their front door. When Germany invaded Poland, Britain announced a declaration of war against Germany. Churchill was the right man, at the right time, and in the right place to be the standard bearer for England and free people everywhere.

Winston—His Early Education

Let's go back in time and examine the life and influences that molded the man who stood as the lone sentinel in the midst of a European community that was crumbling to the overwhelming forces of the Nazi regime. Winston Churchill was born with red hair in 1874 in England to Lord Randolph Churchill and Jennie Jerome. Winston's father, Randolph Churchill, was a son of the Duke of Marlborough, an aristocrat who made his home at Blenheim Palace. Jennie Jerome was an American citizen who lived in New York and was the daughter of Leonard Jerome, a wealthy investor tycoon. She was considered a very beautiful woman in the elite social of New York society. As a result of this marriage, Winston was born into a very wealthy family. In spite of the economic stability that this wealth afforded him, he was determined to make his own way in life.

In polite English society, children were often raised and nurtured by a nanny rather than their mother and father. In Winston's case, his nanny was a woman by the name of Mrs. Everest. As a young child, it was said that Winston was often stubborn and did not respect authority. In spite of the fact that Winston was a most difficult child, Mrs. Everest found ways to nurture his interests, which influenced him greatly in later life. One of these passions was Winston's interest in toy soldiers. He rounded up over 1,500 specially hand carved soldiers and played war games with them. Considering the long line of soldiers in his family tree, Winston's interest in soldiers and war games was a probable and predictable outcome.

Winston's record, at the elite private schools that he attended as a young boy, was marked by disregard for authority; constant argument with the headmasters; and continually getting into trouble. This unruly behavior caused him to spend many hours in the headmaster's office where he was caned/flogged. Although he demonstrated an exceptional memory, his academic record at these schools was unremarkable. Upon leaving Harrow, the last of three private schools he attended, his parents eventually decided to send him to Sandhurst, the military college equivalent to the American West Point. Winston finally passed the entrance exam for admittance to Sandhurst on his third attempt. The purpose of this transition was to provide some structure in their son's life and to support his strong interest in all things military. It was during his years at Harrow and Sandhurst that he developed a command and mastery of the English language and an affinity for debate and discussion. These communication skills, not his mediocre academic record, would serve him well in his emerging public career. In spite of a minor speech impediment, which he learned to manage, it was his oratory and writing skills that would provide Churchill a means to earn a living throughout his life.

A Journalist & Legislator

As a young Army officer and journalist, Churchill and his contemporaries were eager to find war zones in which they could receive recognition and thereby advance their careers. It was 1895 and Churchill sought a posting to Cuba where the Cuban war for Independence (also known as the Spanish-American war) was taking place. Prior to his departure, he arranged with a local British newspaper to compensate him for acting as their war correspondent. This was the first of many such situations that involved Churchill's growing skill in journalism mixed with his career as an army officer. It was during this period of his life that he saw military service in India, the Sudan, and South Africa. In each instance, he was a paid war correspondent for some British newspaper. It was during the second Boer war in South Africa that he was captured; held prisoner; and eventually escaped to become a kind of war hero to the British people. The combination of his notoriety as a war correspondent and his military postings brought the recognition that launched him into a public service career and his first elected position as a Member of Parliament.

It was now 1901 and Winston Churchill was a duly elected Member of Parliament (MP). In those days, members of Parliament served in a voluntary capacity and received no compensation. Most of the income that Churchill earned was from his journalistic and oratory endeavors that took place across England and an extensive speaking tour in the United States. Winston was an excellent speaker and drew large crowds wherever he appeared. As a new Member of Parliament, he quickly began to establish a reputation as one who argued about most every topic including those topics that were presented by his own conservative party. However, Churchill also established a strong reputation as someone who was always hard working; well prepared in his presentations to Parliament; and an exceptional orator. People loved to hear him speak since he used an exceptional vocabulary that enhanced his eloquence as a speaker.

Climbing The Ladder

In 1908, Winston married Clementine Hozier and had four children: Diana, Sarah, Randolph, and Marigold. Of these children, only Randolph followed him into politics. It is interesting to note that Winston's father, Lord Randolph Churchill, had also achieved the rank of a cabinet minister. The highest rank that he reached in the British government was Chancellor of the Exchequer, which his son Winston surpassed when he became Prime Minister.

During his career in government, Winston Churchill held a number of ministerial positions which included: President of the Board of Trade; Home Secretary; First Lord of the Admiralty; Minister of Munitions; Secretary of State for War and Air; Colonial Secretary; and Chancellor of the Exchequer. This broad experience enabled him to connect with many heads of state and prepare him for the greatest job of all: Prime Minister of England.

At the end of World War I, the League of Nations was established in 1920 for the purpose of preventing future wars through a collaboration of nation states. Requirements of the league established a limitation on the size of the German military and, it also established, a fundamental encouragement to all nation states to reduce their military armament. Unfortunately, these requirements became a prelude to World War II. As Germany gradually, and secretly, began to grow its military beyond the limits set by the League of Nations, the nation states of Europe, including Britain, continued to disarm. As a result of Winston Churchill's extensive contacts across Europe, he learned about Germany's secretive growing rearmament. In numerous speeches to Parliament, he warned them about Germany's growing military, but no one believed him. He was branded as a warmonger and ostracized from many elite circles of government.

With the rise of Nazism in the early 1930s and the appointment of Adolf Hitler as Chancellor of Germany in 1933, the European Community slowly began to take notice of a rising threat near the end of the decade. The Prime Minister of England in 1939 was Neville Chamberlain. His policy of appeasement to Germany did not prevent German conquests into Czechoslovakia and Poland. Due to Churchill's overwhelming popularity with the English people and his broad governmental experience in a variety of ministerial positions, Neville Chamberlain offered Winston Churchill the ministerial position of First Lord of the Admiralty in 1939 which he accepted. Within eight months, Neville Chamberlain's policy of appeasement so alienated the English people that Winston Churchill replaced him as Prime Minister in 1940.

The Prime Minister

The British people and the Parliament were now united around the one man who had predicted an approaching war with Germany many years before. It should be stated that France and Britain guaranteed the integrity of European country borders, which were established at the end of World War I with the Treaty of Versailles and each country swore to come to the defense of any nation state should their borders be violated.

It is important to understand the sequence of events that culminated in Winston Churchill becoming the Prime Minister of England. In 1938 Germany invaded and absorbed Austria into the German homeland. This action was taken under the veiled guise of protecting other German-speaking people. In 1939 Germany invaded the area known as the Sudetenland, which was located at the northern border of Czechoslovakia and contained many German-speaking people. Although these aggressive actions alarmed many other European nations, including Britain, no action was taken to stop Hitler's advance. Prime Minister Neville Chamberlain told the Parliament and the British people that these actions were happening in a faraway part of Europe and did not concern England. Within a few months, the countries of Poland, Denmark, Norway, Belgium, and Holland were attacked and occupied by Germany. In May 1940, Winston Churchill became the prime minister of England amid a European Community that was crumbling all around the island of Britain and the only European leader who stood as the lone sentinel against this onslaught. One month after Churchill became Prime Minister, France was attacked and occupied by Germany. This event was particularly notable since France was believed to have had the strongest army in Europe.

Churchill Inspires and Leads

Prior to the time when the United States joined the war in 1941 and was able to bring soldiers and equipment into the battle in 1942-1943, Churchill demonstrated his leadership through the encouragement and hope he brought to Parliament and to the people of Britain. Shortly after the disastrous Battle of Dunkirk, in which the Germans cornered thousands of British and French soldiers against the coast of Calais in France, Churchill delivered a speech to the House of Commons in 1940, which showed the resolve of Britain and its new leader.

> We shall go on to the end, we shall fight in France, we shall fight on the seas and oceans, we shall fight with growing confidence and growing strength in the air, we shall defend our Island, whatever the cost may be, we shall fight on the beaches, we shall fight on the landing grounds, we shall fight in the fields and in the streets, we shall fight in the hills; we shall never surrender, and even if, which I do not for a moment believe, this Island or a large part of it were subjugated and starving, then our Empire beyond the seas, armed and guarded by the British Fleet, would carry on the struggle, until, in God's good time, the New World, with all its power and

might, steps forth to the rescue and the liberation of the old.[2]

Throughout the three month long Battle of Britain in which London and other towns were bombed continuously, the English people looked to their Prime Minister for leadership and he gave it to them. Throughout World War II, Winston Churchill demonstrated his leadership and experience as a prime minister, a statesman, and a strong leader of, not only the British people, but also the people and countries around the world whose freedom had been taken away by Germany, Italy, and Japan—the Axis Powers. His previous experience as First Lord of the Admiralty; Minister of Munitions; and Secretary of State for War and Air brought all of these skills, experiences, and perspectives into the leader who guided the Allies to victory in 1945.

Although Churchill served ably as Prime Minister throughout World War II, he lost his place in the Cabinet in 1945 since the British people were then seeking a peacetime leader. In 1951, he was once again elected Prime Minister and served through 1955.

Some Conclusions about This Leader

In his childhood, Winston Churchill was an undisciplined boy and achieved unremarkable grades at the schools he attended. His early childhood fascination with soldiers and war games became a kind of passion with him,

---

[2] A partial excerpt of a speech delivered by Winston Churchill in 1940, which is referred to as: *We Shall Fight on the Beaches*.

which predisposed him to a career that involved those elements. Another passion of his had to do with mastering the English language in both writing and oratory. The eloquence of his speeches always brought crowds to hear what he had to say. The people that listened to him, whether it was on the street or in the Parliament, were entertained by his eloquence even though they didn't always agree with his strongly held opinions.

Through his journalistic war reporting of his military assignments, he began to be noticed by the people of Britain. His absolute command of the English language set him apart from his contemporaries and provided him with a higher visibility with his electorate. He spoke the truth, as he saw it, and was never intimidated by those in Parliament who called him a warmonger. By the time he was appointed Prime Minister of England, he had served in the military and held several high-level cabinet positions, which gave him a broad base for his leadership of the country. The speeches he gave during the three months of the Battle of Britain, which was probably the lowest point in the morale of the country, gave hope and resolve to all who heard him.

LEADERSHIP ATTRIBUTE MATRIX		
100 points for each category		
1. Integrity		90
2. Risk Taker		100
3. Communication		100
4. Passion		100
5. Vision		100
6. Resiliency		90
TOTAL SCORE for	97%	580
	600 points possible	

Interpretative Lessons for Leaders

- Learn your native language well and be able to write and speak it with eloquence;

- Unremarkable students can become remarkable leaders if they find their passion and build their skill set. There is no known correlation of high academic grades to success in a career;

- Develop a strong and broad foundation of skills before you take on a major leadership position;

- Develop strong social skills and build a network to support you;

- Conduct your research and speak truth to authority;

- Develop your vision and become the chess player so that you can predict the future beyond just two moves

Questions for Reflection

1) What is the quality or attribute in Churchill that took an unremarkable student and created a remarkable leader?

2) Churchill was passionate about saving his country from the armies of Hitler. How would you describe this quality of passion in leadership?

3) How important is it to have a broad experience before taking on a major leadership position? How do you plan to accomplish this in your career?

References

Allen, John. (1945) *Winston Leonard Spencer Churchill in 100 Great lives*. (pp. 472-489) New York: The Greystone Press.

Churchill, Randolph. (1966). *Winston Churchill: Youth 1874-1900*. Boston: Houghton Mifflin Company.

Churchill, Winston S. (1949). *Their finest hour*. Boston: Houghton Mifflin Company.

Delaforce, Patrick. (2012). *Winston Churchill: The great man's life in anecdotes*. England: Fonthill Media Limited.

Gilbert, Martin. (2012). *Winston Churchill: the wilderness years*. NewYork: Tauris Parke Paperbacks.

Johnson, Paul. (2009). *Churchill*. London: Penguin Books.

Taylor, Robert Lewis. (1952) *Winston Churchill: an informal study of greatness*. Garden City, New York: Doubleday & Company, Inc.

Chapter 9

GOLDA MEIR

"I can honestly say that I was never affected by the success of an undertaking if I felt it was the right thing to do, if I was for it, regardless of the possible outcome."[1]

Golda Meir
Prime Minister of Israel

Golda Meir broke the proverbial glass ceiling when she became the first female Prime Minister of Israel in 1969. Her pioneering entrance into the highest levels of Israel's government led the way for notables like Margaret Thatcher, Angela Merkel, and many others to follow within their respective governments in later years. Her political savvy, coupled with her grandmother persona, won the hearts of both American Jews and her own countrymen. She became an international symbol of hope and fairness to oppressed Jews and minorities around the world. Now, let's go back in time and take a look at a few of the factors and influences that prepared Golda Meir to become the Prime Minister of Israel and the most outspoken leader of her country.

---

[1] Enduring words for the leader. 2006

Early Influences

Golda was born in Kiev, Ukraine in 1898 to Moshe Yitzhak Mabovitch and his wife Blume. In spite of the fact that Golda was brought up in a poor Jewish household in an area of Russia that experienced an intense level of Jewish persecution, both her parents were generally optimistic about their life and their opportunities. In her autobiography, *My Life*, Golda recounts that they always had plenty of cousins, as well as, aunts and uncles come to their home. She also sadly recalled that none of them were to survive the Holocaust.

Golda writes in her autobiography that, although she never knew her grandparents, she did know something about them. She describes them both as strong willed people. In particular, her grandmother "...was known for her will of iron and for her bossiness."[2] This characteristic is often attributed to Golda when she served in the various ministries of the government of Israel, including that of Prime Minister.

It was 1906 when 8 year old, Golda, her sister Sheyna, and her mother secretly left Ukraine, using forged documents, to travel to the United States where her father had made a home for them in a poor neighborhood in Milwaukee. During these early school years, Golda learned English and learned to speak without an accent. She enjoyed expressing her opinions and her sense of fairness was always a part of who she was and, eventually, who she became.

---

[2] Meir, *My life*. p. 18.

But it may have all begun for the young Golda, when she was in the 4th grade. In Milwaukee, textbooks were provided to every child for a nominal fee. However, there were many in the poorer neighborhoods that still couldn't afford them. Golda decided to do something about it. She brought together a number of her friends, rented a hall, and planned a Saturday evening to discuss this issue. Dozens of parents attended and witnessed this 11-year old girl delivering an emotional plea that everyone should be treated fairly and all the children needed to have textbooks. By the end of the evening, she and her group had collected a large amount of money, which made it possible for all the students to own their textbooks.

She graduated from the eighth grade and went on to the local high school. However, her parents, who held old cultural values, wanted to arrange a marriage for her with a man who was twice her age. They didn't believe that a young girl needed an education beyond high school and that she should learn the time honored skills of motherhood, homemaking, and cooking. After many arguments, she left home one morning to join her sister, Sheyna, who was already living in Denver. It was during these early teenage years, when she and her sister first learned about Zionism.[3] She attended numerous meetings and connected with many like-minded people who believed in Social Zionism. This was the concept that Zionism, by itself was insufficient as a goal, but the additional belief that many labor and economic wrongs would need to be corrected in order to pro-

---

[3] Zionism is a word that refers to the return of the Jewish people to the land of their forefathers – Israel.

vide a sense of fairness to all. This was not just a mild interest of Golda, it became a passion that consumed her.

She attended many meetings and listened attentively to every speaker, but she did not want to engage in any discussion since she felt lacking in her Yiddish. As she became more confident, she often stood up to express her opinions and hold discussions with her colleagues late into the night. She became deeply committed to the plight of Jews around the world and believed that a Jewish state was the only answer to anti-Semitism. While she was in Denver, she met Morris Myerson who was to become her future husband.

After a time, her father reached out to her and asked her to return home to Milwaukee. She agreed, but with the stipulation that she be able to complete high school and go on to college to become a teacher. While she attended high school, she held part-time jobs so that she would not have to ask her parents for what meager money that the family possessed. During this period of Golda's life in Milwaukee, her commitment deepened as she became more involved in Social Zionism and the Labor Zionist Party. She eventually graduated from high school and began attending the teachers training college. In 1917, she married Morris and decided to leave college since it didn't hold the same interest as the passion that she held for the Social Zionist movement.

A Jewish Homeland

As World War I was coming to a conclusion in 1917, the League of Nations assigned to Great Britain the task of overseeing and governing Palestine. Britain issued the Balfour Declaration, which stated that their objective would be to facilitate the establishment of a Jewish homeland in Palestine.

Golda decided that she wanted to make a difference by actually getting involved in the creation of a Jewish homeland. So in 1921, Golda sold most of her possessions and boarded the *SS Pocahontas* with Morris and departed for Palestine. During the next 3 years, she lived in a traditional Israeli Kibbutz, which was a communal living arrangement with many other people who shared the daily tasks of work. These years gave her first-hand awareness of the need for fairness for all workers.

Golda wanted to do more than simply work in a kibbutz. Opportunities soon became available in which she could represent her kibbutz in larger caucuses and conferences relative to the working conditions in the kibbutz. She eagerly took up issues relating to fairness in working conditions, pay, vacation time, and sick leave. By then, she had acquired a firm command of Yiddish and became just as articulate, as she was with American English. When she spoke to an audience, she seemed to connect with everyone on his or her own level and held a kind of magical power over them while she was speaking. She was both direct and assertive while being sympathetic to the emotions of those who sat with rapt attention to her words. Within a year after leaving the kibbutz, she became recognized as a leader in the Israel Labor Movement.

Golda Enters Politics

Her leadership in the Labor Movement and her command of her audiences brought her to the attention of David Ben-Gurion, who eventually became the first Prime Minister of Israel. Ben-Gurion has often been characterized as the founding father of Israel. Although Palestine was under the protection and management of Britain through the Balfour Declaration, it was trying to grow into a nation state. By this time, the Jewish population in Palestine had increased by 400 percent along with a 200 percent rise in exports. The infant country of Israel still needed many additional resources to energize its manufacturing and small business that it could not provide itself. It was in this environment that Ben-Gurion asked Golda to travel back to the United States and make a plea to the millions of Jewish citizens who held emotional ties to this struggling Jewish settlement.

She drew audiences in Brussels, France, and Great Britain. Golda was viewed, by many, as a kind of international celebrity. In the United States, she drew large audiences and knew how to connect with American Jews, as well as the American public at large. Over the coming years, she made many trips to the United States and always returned with millions of dollars from the pockets of generous Jewish-American citizens who empathized with the plight of this small Jewish settlement in Palestine.

At the conclusion of World War II in 1945, the Allied countries fully learned about the Holocaust and Hitler's final solution. The international community and public opinion were empathetic and supported the United Nations resolution to partition Palestine so that a homeland for the Jewish people could be established. In 1948, Israel formally declared its independence.

In the same year, Golda Meir accepted her first ministerial appointment in the new nation state of Israel by becoming the first ambassador to the Soviet Union. She felt as though she had come full circle and returned to the country in which she was born, but in an elevated status. Her intention was to use that status to let the Jewish population know that there was now a Jewish homeland.

As the Ambassador to Russia, Golda wanted to connect with Russian Jews so she went to the synagogue for Rosh Hashanah services that year. The typical attendance would have ordinarily been around 2,000, but Golda was greeted and surrounded by over 50,000 Jews anxious to meet her. This typified the receptions that she would continue to encounter in other countries. It wasn't just Jewish populations, but also other minorities. To them, she was a voice that would speak to their needs.

During the next 20 years, Golda held various ministerial positions including: Minister of Labor; Minister of Foreign Affairs; and then Secretary-General of the Labor Party. In each of these positions, she distinguished herself as a bold politician and leader in her government. However, she always remained true to her values of fairness for all. Her manner of negotiations with world leaders was always direct and she was never intimidated.

It should be mentioned that, from the very onset of Israel becoming a nation state, Israel encountered Arab threats as a country and terrorist attacks against its citizens.

Their survival as a country was always in jeopardy. Arab countries geographically surrounded Israel and this always posed a tension and the belief that they were indeed alone. The 6-Day War in 1967 was one such attempt to undermine the new Jewish state, which established new borders acquired by Israel during this conflict.

Prime Minister

In 1969, Golda Meir became Prime Minister of Israel and served in that position until 1974. As Prime Minister, Golda cultivated a strong bond and relationship, not only with the American Jewish population, but also with the United States government. The close relationship that she nurtured with President Richard Nixon was a key factor in Israel's survival as a country during the Yom Kippur War of 1973. Israel was in great need of military armaments (including tanks) for defense. Nixon authorized the airlift of the necessary supplies and the state of Israel survived as a nation. When Israel asked for assistance from some European governments, they declined, partly due to their anti-Semitism, and also because they did not want to get involved and risk their supply of oil that was flowing to them from the Arab countries.

Golda Meir handled crisis after crisis while she was the Prime Minister. One instance in particular occurred during the Yom Kippur War when her own ministers failed to properly assess the threat of invasion from the Arab countries and left Israel without a defensive strategy. She delivered a speech to the Knesset, not unlike Winston Churchill's speech during the bombing of Britain in World War II.

She said that Israel would do whatever it must to repel the Arab invaders. She gave hope to the people of Israel who looked to her for leadership.

In 1974, Golda Meir resigned as Prime Minister and four years later passed away at the age of 80. Her legacy lives on as the one person who brought Israel's plight to the attention of world leaders.

Some Conclusions about This Leader

Golda Meir came from poverty, but she directly felt the pangs of persecution and discrimination. This developed in her a sense of fairness and equity that she held as a core value throughout her life. As a young girl and woman, her role models were her mother and her grandmother who were direct and sometimes abrasive in their communication with others.

These early experiences lit a fire within her that would evolve into an unquenchable passion for Social Zionism. She wanted to make a difference and be involved in the establishment of the new Jewish state. To accomplish this, she needed to be able to communicate in both Yiddish and American English. Although she mastered both languages and became a powerful speaker, which attracted large audiences, she never was considered an eloquent speaker. Golda reached her audiences through passionate direct conversations about their needs and, thereby, reaching them on an individual level.

As a minister in the Israeli government, she built a strong and personable network of power brokers she met in her travels around the world. It was this network, which gave her access to those who would help Israel in their time of need. Her sense of fairness; her passion for making a difference; and her command of two languages built a career for her as a world leader in a paternalistic society.

LEADERSHIP ATTRIBUTE MATRIX		
100 points for each category		
1. Integrity		100
2. Risk Taker		90
3. Communication		100
4. Passion		100
5. Vision		80
6. Resiliency		100
TOTAL SCORE for	95%	570
		600 points possible

Interpretative Lessons for Leaders

- Learn your native language well and be able to write and speak it with authority and empathy;
- Learn the art of public speaking;
- Find a passion in your life and follow it;
- Develop a strong foundation of multiple skills before you take on a major leadership position;

- Develop strong social skills and a network to support you;
- Never under estimate your opposition;
- Follow your dream, not the dreams of others

Questions for Reflection

1) Does the experience gained from multiple jobs increase your leadership skills? Why? How would you describe Golda's job preparation?

2) Do you know any great leaders from your past, who reached the top of their profession and lacked public speaking skills?

3) Even though Golda was the Prime Minister of Israel, she failed to properly manage her ministers. What did she do wrong? What would you have done, if you were in her position? Explain your thoughts.

References

Avner, Yehuda. 2012. *The prime ministers: an intimate history of Israeli leadership*. New Milford, CT: The Toby Press.

Burkett, Elinor. 2008. *Golda*. New York: Harper Collins Publishers.

Enduring words for the leader. 2006. Columbus, Ohio: School Specialty Publishing.

Meir, Golda. 1975. *My life*. New York: G.P. Putnam's Sons.

Chapter 10

NAPOLÉON BONAPARTE,
Soldier and Emperor

"Napoléon Bonaparte, certainly the most extraordinary person who has appeared in modern times, and to whom, in some respects, no parallel can be found, if we searched the whole annals of the human race..."[1]

> Lord Brougham
> *Statesman at the time of George III (1778-1868)*

The military genius of Napoléon Bonaparte has not been seen since the time of Alexander the Great, over 20 centuries earlier. He captured the aspirations of the French people by bringing order out of chaos and, through his multiple victories on the battlefield, he brought pride back to the French people. Who was this man? What leadership qualities did he possess that the mere mention of his name brings forth feelings of both respect and revulsion to the people of Europe and Asia? A closer look at Bonaparte will allow the reader to answer these questions in this chapter.

---

[1] Wale. (293)

A Native of Corsica

Napoléon Bonaparte was born on 15 August 1769 at Ajaccio on the island of Corsica, which is located west of the Italian Peninsula in the Mediterranean Sea. The island's culture, language, and government had a strong Italian influence for many centuries until France took control of the island in 1769. This meant that Napoléon became a French citizen in the year of his birth.

Napoléon was one of 13 children born to Carlo and Letizia Buonaparte (*Italian spelling*). Due to Carlo's collaboration with the French after their occupation of the island of Corsica, and some rather questionable documents attesting to his Corsican nobility, Carlo was accepted into the French aristocracy. Even as a minor French noble, he was eligible to have his children educated at French schools. He received scholarships for his children by providing evidence that he lacked the necessary financial resources to properly educate them and also through the intervention of one of his friends in the French aristocracy.

A French Education

At the age of nine, Napoléon was sent to a school at Brienne, France. He was a young Corsican boy sent off to a foreign country to learn a new language. During his school years, and for that matter, during his entire life, he spoke French with a strong Corsican accent. The fact that he did not come from wealthy nobility and that he spoke with a strong accent made him the target of teasing and bullying from his classmates. He was constantly involved in fights and, as a result, he had few friends and became a loner. He handled this social rejection by retreating into a world of books. At Brienne, students were taught many of the basic subjects, including mathematics, and history. These were the two subjects in which Napoléon excelled. He was voracious in his reading—in particular—the military heroes of antiquity.

At the age of 15 in 1784, Napoléon left Brienne and traveled to Paris to attend the elite military school *Ecole militaire* where he would begin his studies in his chosen field as an artillery officer. Although the purpose of this school was to teach students about the art of war and military fortifications, there were no courses offered in military strategies or tactics. Napoléon supplemented his education in these two subjects through his own intense research and extensive reading. This self-taught learning in strategy and tactics proved to be a significant advantage to him on his future battlefields.

Commissioned a 2nd Lieutenant

Upon the early death of his father at age 39 in 1785, Napoléon applied to leave *Ecole militaire* since he was now expected to be the main source of income for his family. At the age of 16, and in that same year, he was granted a commission as a 2nd Lieutenant. Napoléon reacted to his father's death in a rather stoic manner. He felt that his father embarrassed him with his casual and irresponsible life style. However, his affection and devotion for his mother was quite the opposite. He sought counsel from her throughout his life. During the next several years, he had some minor postings to Valence and Auxonne. During these years he honed his skills as an artillery officer and developed an extensive network of political and military contacts, which played a large part in leveraging his rapid military promotions.

It is important to briefly describe the conditions that led to the storming of the Bastille and the French Revolution of 1789. This chaotic environment would create unexpected opportunities for Napoléon. After many decades of war with England, the economy of France was on the brink of collapse. France's treasury was drained and the financial assistance that was given to the struggling Americans, in support of their Revolution, may have been the proverbial straw that broke the camel's back. The imposed entitlements of the monarchy and the aristocracy, along with the spread of the enlightenment across Europe, became significant factors of discontent among the French people.

An Opportunist

Since Napoléon was an officer in the service of his country when the French Revolution erupted, he was considered a royalist—a supporter of the monarchy. It was for this reason that when King Louis XVI and his Queen, Marie Antoinette, were executed, he switched over to the side of the revolutionists. Napoléon was always the opportunist and looked for conditions that would advance his career.

Since many French officers were considered a part of the aristocracy and therefore risked being labeled as a royalist and a possible sentence of death, thousands sought refuge out of the country in order to escape the Reign of Terror. This exodus of talented officers presented situations that were ripe for the opportunist. Such a situation was about to present itself which would introduce Napoléon to the people of France. With the prospect of a general war in Europe, Napoléon was promoted to Captain.

The very act of executing the King and Queen of France threatened the other European nations whose governments were also based upon a monarchy. In 1792, Austria became the first nation to wage war against the new French revolutionists, due in part to the fact that Austria's ruling monarchs were the parents of Marie Antoinette. In 1793 Austria was soon joined by Britain, Holland, and Spain in a coalition to assist the royalists and retake France from the revolutionists led by Robespierre and the Jacobin Club. Austria and their coalition partners reinforced the royalists who had captured Toulon, one of the most impregnable cities in Europe. The French army was weak, partly as a result of the exodus of officers, and lacked the necessary training and battle savvy to retake Toulon.

Prior to this time, Napoléon began to straddle the line between the military arena and political arena. He published a pamphlet entitled: *Le Souper de Beaucaire*, which was a call for national unity, at a time when France was in a state of chaos. This pamphlet brought attention to Napoléon and his expertise as an artillery officer. The Revolutionary Committee of Public Safety ordered Bonaparte, who they promoted to Major, to come to Toulon and direct artillery operations to retake Toulon. With his expertise in siege warfare and the effective use of artillery, Toulon was retaken. Bonaparte played a large part in retaking Toulon and all of France now knew his name. As a result of his actions at Toulon, he was promoted to Brigadier General, and given command of the Paris National Guard, while skipping over the rank of Colonel.

The General Takes Charge

In August 1795, a new French constitution was put into force to replace the monarchy, which created two elected legislative chambers—the Council of Elders and the Council of 500. A Directorate was also formed with five directors elected by these two chambers. In October, a mob of royalist sympathizers approached the Tuileries Palace, the headquarters of the revolutionary government. Their purpose was to bring down the government and restore the monarchy. As the commander of the Paris National Guard, General Bonaparte prepared to defend the palace with his artillery. One of Napoléon's core beliefs was that artillery should bring fear and terror to an opposing force to weaken their resolve. His artillery unit employed this tactic by using cannon grapeshot against the oncoming mob and thereby saved the government. This action, however, killed hundreds of people and seriously wounded many more. However, it also had the effect of ending the Reign of Terror while elevating the name and reputation of Bonaparte. Napoléon had become the hero of the new French Republic.

In 1796 Napoléon Bonaparte married Josephine de Beauharnais and, in that same year, left to participate in the campaign for northern Italy. The Austrians, and their coalition partners, pushed into northern Italy. Through a strategic maneuver devised by Napoléon, the French forces divided the opposing armies and won the day. The French demanded their surrender and an armistice was signed.

During the three years prior to this assignment, he trained his officers and NCOs to read terrain maps and to understand the math associated with the use of artillery. His earlier research on the strategy and tactics of warfare that he learned at *Ecole militaire,* made it possible to more easily defeat his battlefield opponents. His battlefield strategy always sought to divide the opposing army and attack their weakest wing first. The real strength of Napoléon's armies was their speed of attack and their aggressiveness in battle. His army was highly mobile and could move quickly to a preferred battlefield position ahead of his enemy. He fought many battles throughout Europe and used this formula to win almost all these encounters.

During the time known as the Napoléonic Wars (1799-1815), almost every nation in Europe was involved. Napoléon used strict battlefield command structure and battle guidance for his commanders. However, after the battles were won, he allowed his army to loot, pillage, murder, and rape without any oversight. It has been estimated that somewhere between 5-7 million people (includes military and civilian) died during the Napoléonic wars. In order to provide France with funds for their depleted treasury, he taxed the conquered and confiscated their art and their treasures. Much of the art and treasures in the Vatican were taken and sent to France. The looted art treasures and wealth that he presented to the French people made him very popular.

The General Becomes Emperor

Napoléon became so popular with the French people that it became very difficult for the Directory (the five elected leaders under the new constitution) to manage and control his actions. In 1798 Bonaparte brought his armies to Egypt with the intention of crossing over into India to capture this British colony—thus effectively reducing the power of the British Empire. Although the entire campaign ended in disaster for Napoléon, he found the Rosetta Stone which proved to be the key to long lost ancient hieroglyphics.

Napoléon quickly returned to Paris and, through a well-orchestrated political maneuver, he took control of the government and made himself First Counsel. Eventually, in 1804, he crowned himself Emperor of the French People. It was during the next ten years that he established and implemented the Napoleonic Code, which was his most significant legacy. Since Napoléon's conquests stretched across the European continent, the Code had far reaching affects into how governments were to be administered. The Code essentially abolished the feudal system and established a general equality under the law. There are three significant points in the Code, among many others, that should be listed here:

• Allowed freedom of religion
• Government jobs should be based upon merit
• Privileges cannot be based upon birth

Napoléon continued to resist incursions against France and won his greatest victory at Austerlitz in 1805. However, in 1812 Napoléon invaded Russia with a large force of

500,000 and took Moscow, but the harsh winter lead to the death of many of his talented officers and dramatically reduced his army. During the retreat from Russia, he became surrounded by enemy forces and was eventually forced to surrender

Exiled & Escape

In the year 1814, Napoléon abdicated as Emperor of France under the terms of an allied treaty. The Allies came to realize that they were not fighting France anymore, but they were fighting Napoléon Bonaparte. Under the terms of the treaty, he was exiled to the island of Elba where he retained a generous allowance and retained his title of Emperor. Since Elba was only located in the Mediterranean about 12 miles west of Italy, he made his escape to retake his empire in 1815.

The disaster at the Battle of Waterloo finally ended the career of Napoléon and he was sent to the Island of St. Helena which was situated over 1,100 miles west of the coast of Africa and under British jurisdiction. It was there that he died, at the age of 51, in 1821.

Some Conclusions about This Leader

In the novel of the time *Tale of Two Cities*, Charles Dickens writes: "It was the best of times, it was the worst of times..."[2] In that short phrase, Dickens captured the essence of the time and Napoléon made the most of it.

Napoléon began his life in Corsica at a time when he held strong values and ethics. As the French Revolution and the Reign of Terror reached across the country and chaos took the place of order, the ambitious Napoléon became the consummate opportunist. He made a point of appearing humble and, at times, even shy while he let others talk of his accomplishments. He published a pamphlet and other news items to bring attention to himself and what he was achieving.

Napoléon made the most of his early education and supplemented it with his intensive reading. It was this study, which he did on his own that prepared him for a successful career in the military. It was also this self-taught learning, which influenced the writing of the Napoléonic Code that was his greatest legacy.

One of the things he did as a commander was to insure that his army was motivated. He took care of their needs and they stayed with him because they knew that he would continue to win on the battlefield.

Finally, Napoléon was able to gain traction in his career through, what we call today, as networking. He made many friends in both the military and the government that accelerated his career and fed his ambition.

---

[2] Dickens, p. 5

LEADERSHIP ATTRIBUTE MATRIX *100 points for each category*	
1. Integrity	75
2. Risk Taker	100
3. Communication	65
4. Passion	100
5. Vision	100
6. Resiliency	100
TOTAL SCORE for 90%	470
	600 points possible

Interpretative Lessons for Leaders

- Regardless of bullying or how your contemporaries may treat you, know your goals and aspirations and pursue them vigorously;

- Do not boast about your accomplishments; let others do it for you. Based upon what you read in this profile, how would you orchestrate your reputation?

- Develop a network of contacts to accelerate your career.

- Become the expert in your career field and, when you have done that, learn a little more;

- Always take care of those you lead and they will always take care of you.

Questions for Reflection

1) When Napoleon was bullied in school, he retreated to his world of books. It was then that he learned about strategy and tactics that were not taught in his artillery classes. What have you done to learn about your profession- outside of the classroom?

2) Napoléon built a vast network of support in his career. How important is building a network & what have you done to create it in your career space?

3) Have you considered opportunities that were presented to you in your career or did you just stay in your comfort zone? Elaborate.

References

Allen, John. (Ed.). (1945). Napoleon Bonaparte in 100 Great lives. (pp. 415-423). New York: The Greystone Press.

Bowle, John. (1973). Napoléon. Chicago: Follett Publishing Company.

Crofton, Ian. (2006). *George III in The kings and queens of England*. (pp. 199-204). London: Quercus Publishing.

Dickens, Charles. (2004). *A tale of two cities*. (p. 5) New York: Simon & Schuster Paperbacks.

Dupuy, Trevor N., Johnson, C., & Bongard, D. (1995). *Napoléon I in The Harper encyclopedia of military biography*. (pp. 536-538). Edison, New Jersey: Castle Books.

Dwyer, Philip D. (2007). *Napoléon: the path to power*. United States: Yale University Press.

Herold, J. Christopher. (1962). *The age of Napoléon*. New York: Harmony Books.

Johnson, Paul. (2002). *Napoléon*. New York: Viking Penguin, a member of Penguin Putnam Inc.

Lawford, James (1977). *Napoléon: The last campaigns 1813-15*. London: Roxby Press Productions.

Macintosh, James. (1791) *Defense of the French Revolution*. Dublin: W. Corbet

Montgomery, D.H. (1899). *The leading facts of French history*. Boston: Ginn & Company.

Wale, William. (1902). *What great men have said about great men*. (p. 293). London: Swan Sonnenschein & Co.

Chapter 11

CATHERINE THE GREAT,
A Royal Reformer

*"In the history of Russia, she and Peter the Great
tower in ability and achievement over the other 14
Czars and empresses of the 300 year Romanov
Dynasty"[1]*

Robert K. Massie

Catherine II, often referred to as Catherine the Great, began her reign almost 40 years after the more famous Russian Czar, Peter the Great. Although several rulers succeeded Peter, each contributed to erasing the progress he had made. It was Catherine who brought about the Golden Age of Russia and built upon the ideals established by Peter. She brought Russia into the family of European nations and continued his legacy. Catherine's leadership made great strides in reorganizing government institutions; fostering continued education; and significantly expanding Russian territory and commerce by gaining access to the sea.

---

[1] Massie, p.574.

Sophia—The Early Years

Catherine II was born on May 2, 1729 in Stettin, Prussia (now Poland) and given the name Sophia Augusta Fredericka. Her father, Christian Augustus, was a prince of a small German-speaking territory known as Anhalt-Zebst who primarily gained notoriety as a result of his military career. Christian was an honest and somewhat reclusive man who was frugal with his money. Her mother, Johanna Elizabeth, who was a princess in the Holstein-Gottorp family, was the opposite of her husband. She was outgoing and extravagant in her spending and very ambitious. As we will see in Sophia's later life, she took on many of the characteristics of her mother.

Johanna was disappointed in the birth of her daughter since she desperately wanted a son who she could use to leverage herself into the higher ranks of the Prussian aristocracy. Eighteen months after the birth of Sophia, a son was born with the name of Wilhelm Christian. Johanna ignored her daughter and poured all of her affection and tenderness toward her son. This extreme favoritism made a permanent imprint on young Sophia for which she never forgave her mother. Wilhelm turned out to be a weak and sickly child who passed away at the age of twelve.

During the 18th century, the children of nobility were provided with a broad education. Sophia had a governess; equestrian and dancing instruction; special language and other tutors; and religious instruction. In addition, she was taught the French language which was considered to be the language of the nobility and the courts of Europe. Sophia desperately wanted to be liked and appreciated for her intelligence. She discovered that people liked to talk about themselves and all she had to do was listen and ask questions. It was a simple formula and it worked for her throughout her life.

The Grand Duchess

At the age of 14, Sophia and her mother were invited to travel to Russia to meet Empress Elizabeth, the daughter of Peter the Great. The Empress was seeking a wife for Peter Ulrich, her nephew, and the grandson of Peter the Great. She felt that such a match would produce a direct heir to the throne and secure her legacy and guarantee stability in Russia.

Peter Ulrich, the intended husband, was one year older than Sophia and her second cousin. He was a shy and sickly boy who loved all things German. When Sophia and Peter met in Russia, he immediately announced to her that he loved another woman. Nevertheless, the plans for the wedding moved forward with Sophia renouncing her Lutheran religion and being baptized as a Russian Orthodox while taking the name of Catherine. On August 21, 1745, the couple was married and received new titles: Grand Duke Peter and Grand Duchess Catherine. It was not a happy marriage since the new immature husband preferred to play with toy soldiers; became intoxicated often; and exhibited strong loyalties for Prussia; while indulging himself with a number of mistresses. Catherine contented herself by continuing her education and by reading the *Annals* of Tacitus; Montesquieu's *L'Esprit des Lois* (The Spirit of Laws); and Voltaire's *Essai sur les Moeurs et l'Esprit des Nations* (Es-

say on the Manners and Spirit of Nations).[2] These books
made an impression on Catherine and ignited her ambition
to accomplish something meaningful in her life. However,
this was also the time that Catherine began to invite new
lovers into her life.

Becoming the Empress

As the next 16 years unfolded, Peter's erratic behavior
elicited disapproval from his aunt, the reigning Empress
Elizabeth. Russian citizens and the military also became
aware of his behavior and his popularity declined dramatically. However, the opposite was true of Catherine. She
embraced her new Russian Orthodox religion and developed an extensive network of loyal friends among the
nobility and the military. Catherine deeply loved Russia
and her loyalty to Russia was never in question.

On December 25, 1761, the reigning Empress Elizabeth
died. Grand Duke Peter became Emperor Peter III while
Catherine became the Empress Consort. Peter openly told
his wife that he planned to rule with Elizabeth Vorontsova,
his current mistress. The extreme unpopularity of Peter III
became openly apparent. Massie describes this situation
when he writes:

"Peter had provoked and insulted the Orthodox Church,
infuriated and alienated the army, and betrayed his allies.
Nevertheless, effective opposition still needed a specific
cause around which to rally. Peter himself supplied this

---

[2] Massie p. 168.

by endeavoring to impose on his exhausted country a frivolous new war against Denmark."[3]

After only six months as the reigning Emperor, Peter III was removed from power in a lightening coup d'état orchestrated by Catherine and with the help of the military and many nobles loyal to her.

Empress and Reformer

Catherine II's coronation took place on September 12, 1762 at the age of 32, a short nine months after the death of Empress Elizabeth. She ruled a country of twenty million that was the largest in the world. She was well educated and already familiar with the royal courts of Europe. Catherine's education and her exposure to the Enlightenment, which swept across the European continent, opened her mind to many new ideas. As a reformer, she forbade torture by reasoning that the truth could never be reliably discovered with that approach. She brought reasoning to the justice system by moderating punishments to fit the offense.

She sent her ministers out to the European capitals with the authority to acquire art treasures and bring them back to Russia. As a result, Russia has one of the largest collections of art in the world which is housed in the Hermitage. She also began a correspondence with the French reformer and philosopher Voltaire that continued throughout most of her life. Diderot visited Catherine in Russia, at her invitation, so that she could learn from him. Diderot was a writer and

---

[3] Massie p. 250

a philosopher who co-founded and was the primary contributor to the first encyclopedia.

In 1766, the Empress Catherine initiated a reform and entitled it: *Nakaz* (instructtion). She wanted to review the Russian Legal Code to see where changes could be made in Russian law. She prepared her instructions over a two-year period. Catherine wrote:

> "The laws ought to be so framed as to secure the safety of every citizen as much as possible...Political liberty does not consist in the notion that a man may do whatever he pleases...liberty is the right to do whatsoever the laws allow...The equality of the citizens in that they should all be subject to the same laws."[4]

Catherine called a National Assembly and invited people who were elected from all of the free social and ethnic classes in the country. Although some reforms were implemented, the majority of reforms were never instituted for two reasons: 1) the delegates did not fully understand what was expected of them due to their lack of education; and 2) the nobility could not support many changes since it would bring about the end of serfdom and their way life. Serfs were tied to property and could be bought, sold, and punished as the nobles saw fit to do. Much of the wealth of Russia during this period, was obtained through the labors of its serfs. In the final analysis, Catherine did not want to anger the very nobles who supported her claim to the throne. This need for their support would cost her and Russia the greatest reform of all to her country—the end of serfdom. However, the seed that she planted would mani-

---

[4] Massie p. 346.

fest itself in 1861 when Tsar Alexander II issued a proclamation of emancipation for all serfs. It is interesting to note that Abraham Lincoln issued his Emancipation Proclamation, which freed the American slaves, just three years later in 1863.

Catherine knew that Russian commerce needed an avenue to the shipping lanes. Through wars and conflicts with the Ottoman Empire, she expanded the territory of Russia and increased commerce by gaining access to the Black Sea. The new trade routes significantly increased the prosperity of Russia.

Catherine the Great was a reformer Empress and made many significant changes in Russia through her vision and leadership. She made numerous improvements to the efficiency and representation of local governance, hospitals, and other areas of Russia during her reign.

Catherine the Great died on November 17, 1796, probably from a stroke. Her legacy lives on today as a great Ruler of Russia—second only to Peter the Great.

Some Conclusions about This Leader

Catherine's climb to the seat of power in Russia was not an easy one. She overcame many obstacles in her childhood and found strength in learning. It was this education, and the strength that she derived from it, that prepared her for the momentous decisions that she would make as the empress of Russia.

As a teenage girl, she desperately wanted to be liked. She discovered that people liked to talk about themselves and it was through this observation that she began to listen and engage her friends with questions on subjects of interest to them. As she practiced this skill as a young girl, and throughout her life as an empress, she learned the things that were important to others. This practice probably enhanced her empathy for others and improved her understanding of the justice system.

Since Catherine was not a direct line descendent from Peter the Great, she reasoned that she must develop a network of friends and supporters who would be loyal to her. Her patience and humility during the long reign under Empress Elizabeth, along with her continued education, prepared her for what was to come. She adopted Russia as her homeland, while continuing to expand her network of friends and supporters among the nobles and with the military. All of these things came together when she removed her husband, Peter III from power.

Once upon the throne, she built upon the achievements of Peter the Great. Her vision for the future of Russia was second only to the Russian legend: Peter the Great.

LEADERSHIP ATTRIBUTE MATRIX 100 points for each category		
1. Integrity		80
2. Risk Taker		90
3. Communication		80
4. Passion		100
5. Vision		100
6. Resiliency		100
TOTAL SCORE for	92%	550
		600 points possible

Interpretative Lessons for Leaders

- Learn and practice the power of questions so that you can learn about what is important to others. Leadership is more about listening;

- It is alright to be ambitious, but learn the skills that will support that ambition;

- Learn the skills of oral and written communication;

- Develop a network of loyal friends and associates who will support you when you need them;

- Once in a position of power, use it to move the organization forward with vision and great ideas;

• It does not matter what your place may be in the society in which you were born. You are only limited by the limitations you place upon yourself.

Questions for Reflection

1) Catherine learned to use the communication technique of questions to learn and protect herself? Why do you think questions are more powerful than statements? Explain.

2) Why did Catherine build a network of supporters? What was the value for her? Why is it important for you to build a network? Do you have your own network? How do you plan to build it?

3) How does continued learning fit into the leadership equation? How would it benefit you in your career?

References

Allen, John. (Ed.). (1945) *Catherine the great, empress of Russia in 100 Great lives*. (pp. 175-181). New York: The Greystone Press.

Oldenbourg, Zoe. (1965). *Catherine the great*. New York: Random House, Inc.

Haslip, Joan. (1977). *Catherine the grea*t. New York: G.P. Putnam's Sons.

Massie, Robert K. (2011). *Catherine the great: Portrait of a woman*. New York: Random House Trade Paperback Edition.

Canning, John. (Ed.). (1985). *Robert Greacen in Catherine II the Great in 100 great kings, queens, and rulers of the world* (pp. 509-515). New York: Hamlyn Publishing Group Ltd.

Chapter 12

DR. MARTIN LUTHER KING, JR.,
An American Reformer

"Ultimately, a genuine leader is not a searcher
for consensus but a molder of consensus."[1]

Martin Luther King, Jr.

An Overview of the Era

Slavery existed in the United States for well over 200 years before the start of the Civil War. Although President Abraham Lincoln's Emancipation Proclamation in 1863 was a milestone, which led to the eventual demise of slavery, there was still a long and dangerous road ahead for the Negro.[2] Laws were enacted in the southern states to impede the

assimilation of former slaves into the fabric of American culture. The U.S. Supreme Court case of *Plessy v. Ferguson* in 1896 underscored the right of this Supreme Court

---

[1] King, Martin Luther. *The Autobiography of Martin Luther King, Jr.* p. 331.

[2] Negro—a term used to denote African-Americans in that era and by Martin Luther King and the authors cited in the References Section to this chapter.

decision to continue their discrimination of the Negro under the concept of "separate but equal." In other words, as long as southern institutions provided equal accommodations to both blacks and whites, justice was served. Of course, the separate accommodations were never equal! This Supreme Court ruling emboldened southern states and jurisdictions to restrict voting rights; limit housing accommodations; enforce separate schools; restrict theater attendance; separate drinking fountains; prevent marriages between blacks and whites; and require separate rail car accommodations. These are the very freedoms that are taken for granted today. Along the way, the Ku Klux Klan (KKK), and other terrorist organizations intimidated and murdered many Negros. Segregation was rigidly enforced in the southern states through a system of biased courts and law enforcement agencies. This was the era in which Martin Luther King, Jr., the Nobel Prize winning civil rights activist entered this world.

Martin's Formative Years

Michael Luther King, Jr. was born on January 15, 1929 in Atlanta, Georgia to Michael Luther King, Sr. and Alberta Williams King. Although Michael was his given name at birth, his father, a devout preacher, changed his own name and his son's name to "Martin" after their historical namesake Martin Luther. Martin came from three generations of preachers and, it was generally thought that he too, would also follow that path.

Both of Martin's parents were fortunate enough to attend local high schools and receive a college education. His mother instilled in Martin a sense of pride and self-confidence. While his father was active in the local NAACP[3], he was actively engaged in social reform where he could make a difference. As an outspoken pastor in the local Ebenezer Baptist Church, the senior King garnered immense respect from the Negro community. Martin grew up with parents who provided a strongly affectionate family relationship that nurtured his development.

There was one incident that deserves mention here since it helped to shape Martin Luther King, Jr.'s character. In Martin's autobiography, he relates a story about he and his father riding in a car when his father accidently drove through a stop sign. As the story is told, a policeman pulled up alongside their car and asked to see my father's driver's license while using the term "boy" as a form of address. Martin's father replied: "Let me make it clear to you that you aren't talking to a boy. If you persist in referring to me as a boy, I will be forced to act as though I don't hear a word you are saying."[4] Apparently, the police officer was so surprised that he quickly wrote out the ticket; gave it to his father; and departed. This incident did not go unnoticed by his son.

At the age of 15, Martin entered Morehouse College as a freshman. He was drawn to literature and philosophy. It was during this period that Martin read Henry David Thoreau's essay on "Civil Disobedience" which triggered in him an exhaustive search for ways to change the society in

---

[3] NAACP – the National Association for the Advancement of Colored People
[4] *The Autobiography of Martin Luther King, Jr.* p. 8.

which he lived. Four years later, Martin enrolled in the Crozier Theological Seminary in Chester, Pennsylvania.

While he was at Crozier, he began a serious study of the
various ethical and social philosophers, which included:
Plato, Aristotle, Hobbes, Bentham, and Locke. His intel-
lectual quest became one of passion as he searched for a
theoretical model and practical approaches to remove the
evil he saw in society and change it for everyone. It was
during this phase of studies, that he came across the writ-
ings of Gandhi. He was drawn to the philosophy of Gandhi
and his resistance to authority by employing a nonviolent
approach.

As a student at a northern institution of learning, Martin
became very aware of the Negro stereotype. Some of the
characteristics of the stereotype included: being late to
class; having a messy dormitory room; and always sloppy
in one's attire. While he was a student at Crozier, he made
sure that he did the exact opposite of these characteristics.
This also explains why, in his later life, he was always
impeccably dressed. He also excelled in his ability to debate and speak publicly on a number of topics. This was the
period of time when Martin became more pronounced in
expressing his beliefs.

At the age of 22, Martin Luther King, Jr. enrolled in
Boston University's school of theology. It was at this point
in his life that he decided to become a preacher as his life's
work. Boston University gave him the opportunity to continue his studies in Philosophy while engaging in a deeper
dive into theology.

It was while he was a student at Boston University that he met his future wife, Coretta Scott. She was a native of the south from Marion, Alabama. Martin describes her as: "In knowing her, one soon detects that she is a person of courage, determination, and amazing internal strength."[5] Although she was always concerned for his safety, she never restricted his activist activities. She was as much invested in and supportive of the civil rights movement as he would come to be in later years of his life. In the spring of 1954, after receiving his doctorate from Boston University, Dr. Martin Luther King, Jr. and his wife Coretta, set out for Montgomery, Alabama to begin his new job as pastor of the Dexter Avenue Baptist Church. His life was about to change in a most dramatic way.

Dr. King Becomes a Civil Rights Activist

With a high level of excitement and an equal amount of energy, the reverend Dr. Martin Luther King and his wife traveled to Montgomery, Alabama to assume the position as pastor of his first church congregation. Since he believed it was his mission to work with the whole individual, both religious and social, he urged everyone in his pastorate to register to vote and to join the NAACP. In Montgomery, "...50,000 blacks feared the arbitrary power of 70,000

---

[5] King, Martin Luther. *The Autobiography of Martin Luther King, Jr.* p. 37.

whites."[6] Of the 50,000 blacks, only 2,000 were actually registered to vote.[7]

About a year after King arrived in Montgomery, Rosa Parks, a black woman, was arrested for defying the bus segregation laws in that city by sitting in the first seat of the bus. It was the law in Montgomery, and practiced in other cities throughout the south, that the first four seats in any bus were reserved for white passengers. Also, if the bus was full of black passengers and there were no seats available for white passengers who entered the bus, the black passengers must standup and give their seats to the white passengers. She refused to give up her seat and, consequently, was arrested and taken to jail. It must be understood that a dozen other blacks attempted to flaunt the law in the past years, but each time they felt the sting of the law that upheld their white segregationist's culture. In May of 1954, the U.S. Supreme Court ruled in *Brown v. Board of Education* that the "separate, but equal" concept in law could not be achieved. It now became the law of the land that equal treatment is meant for all.

The arrest of Rosa Parks seemed to occur at the right time; at the right place; and with the right people to make a difference. Ralph Abernathy, another pastor who was to become Martin Luther King's closest friend, established the Montgomery improvement Association (MIA). Largely due to Martin's powerful and socially conscious sermons delivered to his congregation, Martin was elected as the first chair of the MIA. With Martin's leadership and a very loyal

---

[6] Lewis, p. 59.
[7] Lewis, p. 59.

following, the MIA established a boycott of the entire bus system in Montgomery. Blacks all over the city volunteered their cars to transport people to their jobs so they would not need to take a bus. During the first 60 days of the boycott, King was arrested for a speeding ticket and taken to jail. A short time later, his house was dynamited and fortunately, his wife and daughter were unharmed. King, true to his belief, advocated non-violence to his followers.

In February 1956, Martin Luther King and his MIA Board were arrested for breaking the anti-boycott law. King was held personally liable for leading the boycott and fined $500 and given 365 days in jail. With a great deal of national media attention focused on Montgomery, the case was appealed. On November 13, 1956, the U.S. Supreme Court affirmed that the Alabama state laws, requiring segregation on a bus, were unconstitutional. The decision ended the first of many confrontations that King would endure throughout his relatively short life.

An International Symbol of Hope

King met with over 100 black leaders in Atlanta during the following January. With the success of the Montgomery bus boycott behind them, these leaders wanted to form a regional group that would move forward toward full implementation of the Supreme Court decision throughout the southern states. They formed the Southern Christian Leadership Conference (SCLC) and asked King to become their President. SCLC recognized that voter registration was the key to bringing about civil rights for the black community, which had been denied them for over two centuries.

In the following year, *Time Magazine* published a cover story about Dr. Martin Luther King, Jr. and the events in Montgomery. He immediately became the symbol of hope for the Civil Rights Movement. He soon began receiving invitations from groups all over the world to visit their countries to talk about the civil rights struggle. In an effort to inspire others to join the struggle for their civil rights, he visited Ghana, India, Italy, France, Nigeria, Egypt, Israel, England, and many cities in the United States. During this year, history also records that President Dwight Eisenhower used federal troops to force integration of the Little Rock Central High School in Arkansas. Full acceptance of the black community into the white culture was not going to be easy.

King soon became a target for death threats; intimidations; and bombings. While autographing his new book: Stride Toward Freedom in Harlem, a crazed black woman struck him with a knife. During the next few years, he was arrested for violating an anti-boycott law; jailed for lunch counter sit-in demonstrations; and other minor traffic offenses. Through all of this, he remained strong and committed to leading the African-American community to civil rights equality.

King was not alone in his fight for civil rights, but was joined by many black and white ministers and thousands of people from both the white and black communities. He was the face of the civil rights movement and he communicated with other organizations, which were formed for the same purpose. One significant group was the Student Nonviolent Coordinating Committee (SNCC). Being a leader was not easy since there were many groups to coordinate and he had to build a united case for action. They decided on a new strategy for Birmingham, Alabama. Instead of confronting the white establishment for full civil rights recognition, they needed leverage. In Montgomery, they successfully boycotted the buses that hurt the bus companies and their operating revenues. They needed to do something similar in Birmingham. It was now April 1963 and they decided to boycott the merchants during the Easter holidays.

The boycott and the non-violent demonstrations were massive and led to the incarceration of hundreds in the African-American community, including Martin Luther King. While in jail, Martin penned his now famous *Letter from Birmingham Jail*. It was addressed to his fellow clergymen who were becoming very disheartened with the entire boycott strategy with so many of their community being sent to jail. King's letter put everything into perspective for them and told them that: "...freedom is never voluntarily given by the oppressor, it must be demanded by the oppressed."[8] King further writes: "A social movement that only moves people is a revolt. A movement that changes both people and institutions is a revolution."[9] In the summer of 1963, Martin Luther King orchestrated a march into Washington D.C. to bring the issue of racial discrimination to the forefront. This revolutionary march led to King's *I have a Dream* speech in front of the Lincoln Memorial. Although President Kennedy proposed new civil

---

[8] King, Martin Luther. *The Autobiography of Martin Luther King, Jr.* p. 191.

[9] King, Martin Luther. *The Autobiography of Martin Luther King, Jr.* p. 220.

rights legislation, he was assassinated in November of that year. In July of 1964, ten years after the Supreme Court decision of *Brown v. Board of Education* (*integration to preserve equality*) that over-turned *Plessey v. Ferguson* (*separate, but equal*), President Lyndon Johnson signed into law the Civil Rights Act of 1964. In December of that same year, Dr. Martin Luther King, Jr. received the Nobel Peace Prize and donated the proceeds of that award to the Civil Rights Movement. The voting rights marches in Selma, Alabama eventually led to the Voting Rights Act of 1965. The road to equal treatment under the law had been a long one and full voter enfranchisement, throughout the United States, had still not been achieved by 2016. However, Dr. Martin Luther King, Jr. was at the right place; at the right time; and possessed the leadership skills that started a revolution.

King realized that the cycle of poverty begins with access to a quality education. If a person does not have access to a quality education, he/she cannot make a livelihood outside of the neighborhood in which he/she resides. This cycle becomes demeaning and lowers the person's expectations of becoming a fully productive member of society.

Dr. Martin Luther King, Jr. did not reach the Promised Land that he described so eloquently for his followers. Instead, on April 4, 1968, someone who could not handle the concept of equal rights for everyone, assassinated the shepherd of the Civil Rights Movement at the age of 39.

Some Conclusions about This Leader

There is so much that can be learned from this leader. First of all and maybe the most obvious, a leader does not need to have positional authority in order to lead. He was not the leader of a conventional organization that was fully funded and staffed, but the leader of a loosely formed association with very little funding. His passion for addressing the entire person, including both spiritual and social, attracted many followers to his cause. In other words, find your passion; develop your commitment; and move forward toward your goal.

Prior to accepting the mantle of leadership, he educated himself so that he would understand how others handled similar issues in history. He wanted to conduct exhaustive research about similar events in history and learn from them.

Although he was sensitive to consensus building, he recognized that a leader actually molds the consensus and builds it through the leader's conviction. He learned from his mistakes and adjusted his strategy as he moved forward. He concluded that he could achieve his goal more quickly if he would only select one element of the grander strategy on which to focus. Finally, he motivated his followers with a grand dream that was bigger than he was. As a result, African-Americans enrolled themselves into his dream.

LEADERSHIP ATTRIBUTE MATRIX
100 points for each category

1. Integrity	100
2. Risk Taker	100
3. Communication	100
4. Passion	100
5. Vision	100
6. Resiliency	100
TOTAL SCORE for 100%	600
	600 points possible

Interpretative Lessons for Leaders

- Learn how to communicate both orally and in writing;

- Value learning and that learning will give you confidence;

- Motivate your workforce with a goal/grand vision that would benefit all of your followers;

- Devise a strategy that points a laser at an element of the larger goal;

- Mold and build a consensus from your passion and convictions;

- Keep your eye on the prize and don't let obstacles keep you down;

- A leader can lead from any base of authority or commitment. A leader does not need to be anointed as a leader from a position of authority, but can lead from his/her passion and commitment;

- Build your network. You cannot lead without followers.

Questions for Reflections

1) Does a leader build a consensus from a group or does the leader mold a consensus from convictions? Explain. What did King do?

2) When considering change in your organization, why is it important to point a laser at a small change first? Explain from the point of view in King's profile.

3) What did you learn from King's life? Why is it important to build a strong network to lead?

References

Carson, Clayborne. (Ed). (1998). *The auto biography of Martin Luther King, Jr.* New York: Grand Central Publishing.

Lewis, David L. (1978). *King: a biography.* Chicago: University of Illinois Press.

Suriano, Gregory R. (Ed). (1993). *Great American speeches.* pp. 239-243. New York: Random House Publishing, Inc.

Chapter 13

MARGARET THATCHER,
The Iron Lady of the West

"I do not know anyone who has got to the top without hard work. That is the recipe. It will not always get you to the top, but it should get you pretty near." [1]

Margaret Thatcher
Prime Minister of the United Kingdom

Lady Margaret Thatcher came from humble beginnings in a small town outside of London and rose to become the longest serving Prime Minister of England during the 20th century. She was the first female Prime Minister of the western world who served her country during a precarious period in world history referred to as the Cold War. The

Berlin Wall, which separated East Germany from West Germany for 28 years, collapsed in 1989 due to the leadership of three world leaders: Ronald Reagan, Margaret Thatcher, and Pope John Paul II. These three world leaders each played a role from their own unique field of influence. The significance of this event brought the governments of the world a little closer into a world community.

---

[1] Blundell, p. 192

Margaret Finds her Compass

Margaret Roberts was born on October 13, 1925 in the town of Grantham within the United Kingdom. Her father was Alfred Roberts who owned a small grocery store in the same building in which they lived. Her mother, Beatrice Stevenson, was an accomplished dressmaker who also owned a small business. Muriel, Margaret's older sister by four years, was born in 1921. Margaret's modest beginning was evidenced by the fact that the flat, in which they lived, had no bath or running hot water. The Roberts family was one of many small businesses across England that struggled to make ends meet. It was during these early years that she learned the value of hard work, reliability, and preparation. It was these qualities that she learned as a young girl that would serve her well as a prime minister in her later life.

While attending grade school, she learned to play the piano and became confident in reciting poetry out loud to anyone who would listen. This, of course, led her to enter a number of poetry recital contests. "When a teacher implied that Margaret had been "lucky" to win the recital prize, the 10-year-old gave her a lecture on the value of hard work and preparation.[2] It was this kind of early activity that would give Margaret the experience and confidence to develop her public speaking ability.

From her mother, she learned how to save money; manage a household; and organize her time around multiple tasks. From her father, she learned some of the philosophy and attributes which would provide the driving compass

---

[2] Bundell, p.21.

throughout her life. Her father taught her not to alter her convictions just because others may disagree with her. He taught her to hold her position, in the light of opposition, if she knew she was right.

In October 1943, Margaret entered Oxford University to study chemistry to become a scientist. Although she felt that this would become her life's work, she was about to be exposed to politics when her father became an Alderman and eventually a Mayor of the local Borough (1945-1946). By this time, she had become an active member of the Oxford University Conservative Association (OUCA). This was the time in her life when she began to turn away from chemistry as a career and focus upon an emerging political life. As an active member of OUCA and its debating club, she developed her early political network and participated in a number of debates and public speaking events.

Entry into the Political Arena

In 1947, Margaret Roberts left Oxford University with a degree in Chemistry and eventually secured a job with BX Plastics. During the next 12 years, she built her foundation for her entry into politics. Soon after she began work as a research chemist, she also became a member of the local Conservative Party. It was during this time that she met and married her husband, Denis Thatcher, who was to become her political confidant throughout her career. After a time, she switched her career to law and qualified as a tax barrister. During this transitional period, she gave birth to twins, Mark and Carol. Now, she had a family; a devoted husband who was able to provide advice and counsel in her career; and a developing passion to make a difference in the lives of middle class British citizens. She finally knew what she wanted to do with her life. Now, all she needed was a seat in Parliament.

In 1959, Margaret (Roberts) Thatcher was elected as a Member of Parliament (MP) in the Conservative Party. During earlier failed attempts, she honed her public speaking skills to the point where she attracted hundreds of people wherever she spoke. She was a young and attractive woman who had mastered the art of public speaking. She was now on her way!

Although she was a new MP, she was recognized by the leadership of the Conservative Party as an asset due to her ability to debate and skillfully articulate platform issues. Over the next several years, Margaret Thatcher served in a variety of ministerial positions, which included: Education, Pensions, Housing, Treasury, Transport, and Fuel & Power. Each assignment afforded her a wide spectrum of experience and enabled her to continue to build a vast political network. During her earlier years as a junior MP, she came to realize that her colleagues respected her extensive preparation prior to speaking in front of the Parliament. Her sincerity and passion, observed through her presentations, were valuable assets recognized by her Party.

In 1975, Thatcher was elected to lead the Opposition - Conservative Party. Just four years later on March 4, 1979, the ruling Labour Party failed a vote of confidence and Margaret Thatcher became the Prime Minister of England. She was the first woman in Europe to lead a major party and a government. There were four intervening years in which Edward Heath led the Conservative Party. However, Heath did nothing to change the path that had been previously set by the Labour Party six years earlier.

Rescuing the Country

When Thatcher became Prime Minister in 1979, she inherited three major domestic problems that materialized as a result of 15 years of government leadership by the Labour Party (1964-1978). The three issues facing Prime Minister Thatcher and the Conservative Party included:

1. A recession and high unemployment;
2. The excessive power and influence of trade unions;
3. The budget drain of state owned companies.

All three issues were inter-related. In Thatcher's own autobiography, she writes:

"The root of Britain's industrial problem was low productivity. British living standards were lower than those of our principal competitors and the number of well-paid and reasonably secure jobs was smaller because we produce less per-person than they did."[3]

She believed that a pay or salary standard did not belong in a national government policy platform. The focus of policy needs to be on production and performance. The Prime Minister and her cabinet crafted a policy that produced light deregulation of industry; cut the tax rates; reduced government spending; and lifted the stranglehold of the unions on both employers and trade union members. All

---

[3] Thatcher (2010) p. 298.

of these combined tactics had a positive effect on unemployment and the recession. However, there was more to
be done to bring about the economic stability that she was
seeking.

Prime Minister Thatcher realized that, during the years
that the Labour Party led the government, a number of
companies were nationalized under a socialist agenda that
propagated the idea that companies would perform better if
they were owned by the state. This produced an excessive
economic burden for the British taxpayer. The individual
employee output and high wages, brought about by the
stranglehold of the unions, made British goods uncom-
petitive in the international marketplace.

The Conservative Party, under Prime Minister Thatcher's leadership, divested the government of many enterprises and moved them into the private sector marketplace.
The government's financial tax burden, before divesting
these enterprises, was too immense for the people to bear.
Only a few, of over 30 enterprises[4] that were sold, are listed
below:

> *British Petroleum*
> *British Aerospace*
> *British Telecommunications*
> *British Airways*
> *British Steel*
> *National Freight Corporation*
> *Jaguar*
> *Rolls Royce*

---

[4] Blundell. P. 103.

The Falklands War

Although Prime Minister Margaret Thatcher never expected to be faced with the decision to send British troops to war, her skills and judgment were severely tested with this incident. On March 31, 1982, intelligence reports were received that indicated Argentina was preparing to invade the Falkland Islands.

Some background information is important for the reader to understand the context of the events that were transpiring. The Falkland Islands are located about 500 miles East of the southern tip of Argentina. There was a substantial British presence on the islands for over 150 years and the citizens wanted to remain under the protection of the British Empire. The United Nations charter recognized the principle of self-determination as a fundamental component of international law.[5] In December of the previous year, there was a change in the Argentine government, which placed General Leopoldo Galtieri in as the new president.

In spite of the UN Secretary-General's attempt to restore stability through Security Council Resolution 502, which demanded the immediate withdrawal of Argentine forces, the invasion force proceeded. After creating her War Council and briefing Parliament, Thatcher directed a task force on April 5th to head for the Islands with a military complement of over 25,000 men and 100 vessels.

Although the Prime Minister receives plenty of input from a variety of factions within and outside the govern-

---

[5] Thatcher (2010). p. 340.

ment, the leader is essentially alone when a decision is made. Margaret Thatcher's iron will was honed over the years and she learned to judge a situation and do the right thing.

By June 1982, the invasion was stopped and over 9,500 Argentine soldiers surrendered. Britain had entered onto the world stage and returned victorious while establishing their position in the world order. Margaret Thatcher's political capital just about reached that of Winston Churchill.

The Wall Came Tumbling Down

The Russians, right at the end of World War II, built the wall separating East Berlin from West Berlin. This was the beginning of the 28-year Cold War between Russia and the Western European countries, which included the United States. There was no one person who can be directly linked to bringing down the wall. However, if we were to understand the full context of how the wall came down, we must include the leadership of three world leaders who influenced the opinions of large populations. Ronald Reagan, President of United States; Margaret Thatcher, Prime Minister of the United Kingdom; and Pope John Paul II, the head of the world Roman Catholic Church. Although President Reagan was the leader of the most powerful country in the world, Prime Minister Margaret Thatcher was leader of one of the strongest countries in Europe. She demonstrated to the world how free enterprise can bring freedom to anyone who is willing to work for it. Pope John Paul II's influence over Roman Catholic followers and his intervention in

Poland added to the collective force of these three leaders to bring down the wall.

Margaret Thatcher understood the importance of a free enterprise system and human rights, which enables the system to function. These are her words:

> When the Soviet leaders jail a writer, or a priest, or doctor or a worker for the crime of speaking freely, it is not only for humanitarian reasons that we should be concerned. For these acts reveal a country that is afraid of truth and liberty; it dare not allow its people to enjoy the freedoms we take for granted, and a nation that denies those freedoms to its own people will have few scruples in denying them to others[6]

In 1990, Margaret Thatcher stepped down as Prime Minister, but stayed on as an MP for two more years. In April 2013, she passed away from a stroke and into history.

Some Conclusions about This Leader

Margaret Thatcher was born into a family that valued free enterprise. Her mother taught her how to manage their family budget and organize her time, while her father taught her the value of hard work, reliability, and preparation. She observed her father's campaign for mayor of a small borough outside of London and realized that the skills of public speaking would be a necessary tool in her career.

---

[6] Thatcher (2010). p. 205.

The very skills that she learned as a child brought her the recognition and advancement that she desired in her career. As a junior minister in a cabinet, she rotated to a number of different minister portfolios, which afforded her an unusually broad set of experiences. Along the way, she continued to develop and build her network of friends and associates that helped to advance her career. She became known, by her fellow MPs, for her thorough preparation prior to making any presentation.

Aside from the skills and experiences mentioned above, she developed a passion for making a difference in the lives of middle-class British citizens. The passion she displayed in her work exceeded that of her contemporaries who simply saw their work as a job. Although she had to overcome the prejudice of a woman working in what may be perceived as a male dominated Parliament, she demonstrated her confidence and stood out as a member of Parliament who was well prepared and demonstrated her extremely articulate presentations.

Although she sought advice from her cabinet, she alone made the tough decisions usually against strong head winds to the contrary. Her reputation still stands strong and today her statue in parliament gazes across the open floor to the statue of Winston Churchill.

LEADERSHIP ATTRIBUTE MATRIX 100 points for each category		
1. Integrity		100
2. Risk Taker		80
3. Communication		100
4. Passion		100
5. Vision		100
6. Resiliency		100
TOTAL SCORE for	97%	580
		600 points possible

Interpretative Lessons for Leaders

- Follow your passion and desire to make a difference;
- Learn and practice good public speaking skills;
- Develop a large network of supporters;
- Expose yourself to a variety of jobs or positions so that you can increase your value to an organization. Bring a wide breadth of experience to a leadership position;
- If you know that you are right on an issue, stand firm in spite of the prevailing winds to the contrary. A leader usually stands alone.

- Always come prepared to a meeting—it may set you apart
- Seek advice from your staff, but be prepared to make the hard decisions

Questions for Reflection

1) After a thorough analysis of a situation from your staff on a critical issue and you make a decision, what do you do when a staff person questions your decision? How do you think Thatcher would have handled it?

2) Margaret Thatcher was always thoroughly prepared whenever she made a presentation. What do you think that this practice communicated to her colleagues and the opposing party? Are you always prepared before you make a presentation? Elaborate.

3) Is there someone in your chain-of-command who intimidates you? Why? What can you do to resolve and overcome this intimidation?

References

Blundell, John. (2008) *Margaret Thatcher: A portrait of the Iron Lady*. New York: Algora Publishing.

Phillips, Charles. (2015). *50 Leaders who changed history*. Pp. 196-200. London: Quantum Books Ltd.

Thatcher, Margaret. (1993). *Margaret Thatcher: The downing street years*. New York: HarperCollins Publishers.

Thatcher, Margaret. (2010). *Margaret Thatcher: The autobiography*. New York: HarperCollins Publishers.

Chapter 14
THOUGHTS AND REFLECTIONS

In the first three chapters of this book, the author laid out the premise for writing this book and explored various leadership theories that may help the reader to better understand the concepts of leadership. Chapter 3 listed six leadership attributes and examined their characteristics as they relate to great leadership. The purpose then was to examine the lives of ten great leaders who left their mark in the annals of world history and see if there are any common denominators which would help to explain why they are remembered today as—extraordinary leaders. This knowledge could enrich your own leadership journey as you strive to discover what you need to do to become the best that you can become.

Although the path to becoming a leader is a journey that each of us must travel alone, we can learn from the examples and behavior of these extraordinary leaders. In a similar vein, we can learn from their mistakes so that we will be less likely to repeat them. With this in mind, let us re-examine the **Ten** *Leadership Attribute Matrix* forms that were used to rate each leader against the six same attributes shown below.

INTEGRITY
RISK TAKER
COMMUNICATION

PASSION
VISION
RESILENCY

Of the six Attributes, three of them stood out as the most common attributes of the ten leaders that we profiled. They were:

**PASSION
VISION
RESILENCY**

All ten of the leaders received the maximum number of points for **Passion**. Eight were rated as also possessing a **Vision** and a **Resiliency** as a part of their leadership strategy. A passionate commitment to an outcome, coupled with a grand vision for the leader's followers brings the equation into a proper balance for action. Resiliency recognizes that there will be bumps in every road, but the leader is prepared to get up and move on to the result for which he/she is committed.

The final three attributes are:

**INTEGRITY
RISK TAKER
COMMUNICATION**

Integrity, **Risk Taker**, and **Communication** all received varying degrees of importance by the great leaders from world history. **Integrity** is less about the ethics of the time, but more about the trust that must exist between the leader and the follower. A leader must be a **Risk Taker** because that is the edge between winning and losing. Without a risk, there cannot be a win. Finally, **Communication** is the skill of conveying your passionate commitment to an outcome, as well as your grand vision, to your followers.

All six of the Leadership Attributes are critical to successful and significant leadership outcomes. It is also interesting to note that five of these attributes are learned skills, but only **Passion** is the one attribute that is not learned, but part of the DNA of the leader. Not everyone can reach deeply into themselves and bring out a deep sense of passionate commitment to an outcome. However, the person that possesses it has the glue and that certain something that brings all of the other leadership attributes into focus at a time when leadership may be needed by your organization and our society. A strong **Passion** is the characteristic which triggers the skills of great leaders.

You can become a Great Leader!

- First of all, reflect upon what you have read in this book. Find a field of interest that truly invigorates your spirit. In other words, you need to find something for which you can become passionate to reach a result or make a difference.

- Become an expert in that field. Learn as much about it as anyone within your professional circle. And then, learn a little more.

- Imagine yourself in a leadership position within the field for which you have become an expert. The leadership position should be at least 3-4 levels above where you are in the organization. Study the education and experience level of a person who holds that position for whom you also admire. Make a career plan to obtain the equivalent education and experience level, which will enable you to perform in that position.

- Showing all due respect to that person, reach out and introduce yourself; explain your interest; and invite that person to lunch. See if he/she will mentor you. If not, find someone who will within your field of interest.

- Obtain experience in multiple organizations. It may be uncomfortable at first, but it will give you a wide level of experience and the confidence that will help to propel your career forward.

- Build a professional career network. You cannot become a leader without the support of others.

- Work on all six Leader Attributes described and profiled in this book.

- **Remember this**: arrogance can destroy all that you may have acquired in your career. Be confident, but never arrogant.

You are on your way!

Index

6-Day War, 100
Adjutant General, 68
Adolf Hitler, 79, 85
Ajaccio, 106
Alberta Williams King, 132
Alderman, 147
Alexander Hamilton, 75
Alexander the Great, 27, 35, 39, 40
Alfred Roberts, 146
Anhalt-Zebst, 120
Argentine Government, 142
Aristotle, 29
Augustine and Mary Ball Washington, 66

Balfour Declaration, 97, 98
Barbarism in Russia, 55
Battle of Waterloo, 114
Beatrice Stevenson, 146
Blenheim Palace, 80
Bloody Mary, 45
Blume, 94
Borough, 147
Boston University, 135
British Parliament, 6
Brown v. Board of Education, 136, 140
Bucephalus, 30
BX Plastics, 148

Carlo and Letizia Buonaparte, 106
Catherine of Aragon, 43, 44
Catherine the Great, 119, 125, 126
Chancellor of Germany, 85
Chancellor of the Exchequer, 83, 84
Christian Augustus, 120
Civil Rights Movement, 138, 140, 141
Civil War, 131
Clementine Hozier, 83
Cold War, 145, 153
Colonel Starts a War, 69
Colonial Officer, 67
Communication, 11, 18, 23, 160
Conclusions about each Leader, 23, 35, 49, 61, 75, 88, 101, 114, 126, 141, 154
Conservative Party, 148, 149, 151
Continental Congress, 72, 74
Contingency Leadership Theories, 8
Corsica, 106, 114
Council of 500, 110
Council of Elders, 110
Czar Alexis, 56
Czar of Russia, 56, 59, 60, 61
Czar Theodore (Feodor), 56

David Ben-Gurion, 98
Denis Thatcher, 148
Dexter Avenue Baptist Church, 135
Directory, 112
Doge, 58

Ebenezer Baptist Church, 133
Ecole Militaire, 107, 111
Edward Heath, 149
Elizabeth I, 41, 46, 48, 50, 54
Emperor of France, 113
Empress Elizabeth, 121, 122, 123, 126
English Reformation, 43

Falkland Islands, 151, 152
First Lord of the Admiralty, 84, 85, 88
Fredericksburg, 66
Free Enterprise System, 153
French and Indian War, 68, 69, 70
French Aristocracy, 106
French Revolution, 108, 114, 118

Genghis Khan, 55
George II, King of England, 67
George Washington, 65, 66, 68, 70, 71, 74, 75, 79
Golda Meir, 93, 99, 100, 101
Golden Age of England, 41
Gordian Knot, 32
Governor Robert Dinwiddie, 69
Grand Duchess Catherine, 122

Great-Man Theory, 6

Harrow, 81
Hessian soldiers, 74
Holocaust, 94, 99
Holstein-Gottorp family, 120
Home Secretary, 84

I have a Dream, 140
Integrity, 11
Integrity, 16, 17, 23
Integrity, 160
Interpretative Lessons for Leaders, 24, 37, 52, 63, 77, 90, 103, 116, 128, 143. 156
Island of St. Helena, 114

Jacobin Club, 109
Jennie Jerome, 80
Jewish Homeland, 97
Johanna Elizabeth, 120
Josephine de Beauharnais, 111

Kibbutz, 97
King Darius of Persia, 32
King George III, 71
King Henry VIII, 42, 43
King Louis XVI, 109
King Philip, 28, 31
Kremlin, 58
Ku Klux Klan, 132

Labour Party, 149, 150
Le Souper de Beaucaire, 110
leader, 5, 6, 7, 8, 9, 10, 11, 12

Leadership Attribute Matrix, 23,
  36, 52, 62, 77, 89, 102, 115,
  128, 142, 155
Leadership Attributes, 15
Leadership Theories, 6
leadership, 5-10, 12, 13
Leadership, 89
League of Corinth, 28
Letter from Birmingham Jail,
  139
Lord Randolph Churchill, 80, 83

Margaret Thatcher, 145, 148,
  149, 151-154, 157, 158
Martha Dandridge Custis, 70
Martin Luther King, 131-141,
  145
Mary Queen of Scots, 46, 47
Member of Parliament, 82, 83,
  148
Michael Luther King, 132
Milwaukee, 94, 95, 96
Morehouse College, 134
Morris Myerson, 96
MP, 148, 154

NAACP, 133, 136
Napoléon Bonaparte, 105, 106,
  111, 114
Napoléonic Code, 115
Napoléonic Wars, 112
Natalya Naryshkina, 56
Neville Chamberlain, 85, 86
Nobel Prize, 132
Nonviolent approach, 134

Olympias, 28, 31
Oracle at Delphi, 31
Oxford University Conservative
  Association, 147
Oxford University, 147

Palestine, 97, 98, 99
Paris National Guard, 110
Passion, 11, 19, 20, 23, 160, 161
Peter the Great, 55, 59, 61, 64,
  65, 119, 121, 126, 127
Peter Ulrich, 121
Plessy v. Ferguson, 132
Pope Clement VII, 43
Pope Pius V, 45
President Dwight Eisenhower,
  138
President Lyndon Johnson, 140
President Richard Nixon, 100
Prime Minister of England, 145,
  149
Prime Minister of Israel, 93, 98,
  100, 104
Prime Minister, 79, 84, 85, 86,
  87, 88, 89
Prussia, 122

Queen Anne Boleyn, 42, 49
Queen Mary, 42, 44, 45, 53
Queen, Marie Antoinette, 109
Questions for Reflection, 24, 37,
  53, 63, 78, 91, 104, 116, 129
  144, 157

Resiliency, 11, 21, 22, 23, 160
Revolutionary Committee of
    Public Safety, 110
Risk Taker, 11, 17, 23, 160
Rosa Parks, 136, 137
Rosh Hashanah, 99
Royal commission, 68, 75
Russian Czar, 119
Russian Legal Code, 124
Russian Orthodox, 121, 122

Sandhurst, 81
Satrap, 343, 35, 37
Serfs, 125
Servant Leadership, 7
Sheyna, 94, 95
Significant Reforms, 62
Sir Francis Drake, 48
Situational Leadership, 8
Slavery, 131
SNCC, 139
Social Zionism, 96, 102
Sophia Augusta Fredericka, 120
Sophia, 57
Spanish Armada, 47, 49, 50, 53
Spanish-American War, 82
SS Pocahontas, 97
Stamp Act 1765, 71
Stettin, Prussia, 120
Student Nonviolent
    Coordinating Committee, 139

The Berlin Wall, 145
The Falklands War, 151
Thoughts and Reflections, 159
Toulon, 109, 110
Town of Grantham, 146
Trait Theory, 7
Transformational Leader, 8
Treaty of Versailles, 85
Tsar Alexander II, 125
Tuileries Palace, 110

U.S. Supreme Court, 132, 136,
    137
Valley Forge, 72
Vision, 11, 20, 23, 160
Voltaire, 122, 124

Wilhelm Christian, 120
William Shakespeare, 49
Winston Churchill, 79, 80, 83,
    84, 85, 87, 88, 92
World War II, 84, 87, 88

Yiddish, 96, 97, 102
Yom Kippur War, 101
Yorktown, 74, 79
Zeus, 28, 31